RTI: Assessments &Remediation for K–2

Brenda M. Weaver, Ed.D.

SCHOLASTIC

New York · Toronto · London · Auckland · Sydney
Mexico City · New Delhi · Hong Kong · Buenos Aires

*This book is dedicated to my dear friends,
Winnie and Mike Bixler, for their special friendship,
all of their caring support, and for introducing me to
the wonder and enjoyment of Cairns.*

Acknowledgments

"Mystery of the Missing Cat Food," "Lost in the Snow," and "Jane Goodall and the Chimps,"
were written by Betsy Franco and first appeared in *12 Genre Mini-Books* by Betsy Franco
(Scholastic, 2002). Many thanks to Betsy for allowing them to appear in this book.

Cover design by Jorge J. Namerow

Cover photograph by Ellen B. Senisi

Interior design by Sydney Wright and LDLDesigns

Interior illustrations by Maxie Chambliss

ISBN-13: 978-0-545-16042-1

ISBN-10: 0-545-16042-1

Contents

CHAPTER 14 Intervention Instruction for Writing

APPENDIX

Chapter 1

Introduction

Recently, RTI, or Response to Intervention, has gained significance in the education field. This approach to instruction has always been characteristic of effective teachers, who monitor their students and adjust their teaching to enhance students' learning. This book describes the RTI model and possible implementations, and includes a description of a process teachers and administrators can use to determine the necessary components for an RTI program in their own school. I also devote a chapter to curriculum development, state standards, and state assessments and demonstrate how integrating these components can further increase the effectiveness of an RTI Program. The remainder of the book provides literacy assessments that can serve as a monitoring system for RTI programs.

Assessment: The Key to Monitoring Progress

Assessment is a prerequisite for differentiating instruction and monitoring progress because it identifies students' strengths and needs. We must have specific measures so that what the assessment is telling us will assist us in providing the adjustment in instruction. Many literacy programs have assessments, but they are often incomplete. For example, some programs advance children based on their skills and strategies in oral reading fluency alone. While oral reading fluency is a vital element of literacy, writing and comprehension are also critical to the success of students. We must assess students regularly on all aspects of literacy, so we can address immediately any needs that arise. Otherwise, we risk having students fall behind.

This book contains assessments that clearly identify how students are progressing in all the key areas of literacy in grades K–2. These assessments do not replace teacher observations or informal assessments. Rather, they augment them by providing a snapshot of students' overall literacy development at periodic intervals during the year. Used together, anecdotal notes, informal assessments, and these periodic assessments will give you the information you need to provide appropriate, effective instruction for all students.

Once you have determined the needs of your students through assessment, you need options for instruction. In addition to providing assessments, this book also contains several activities, strategies, and techniques that you can select based on student need (see Chapters 11–14).

A Research-Based Model That Works

The literacy assessments and instructional interventions presented in this book are classroom tested and research proven. They are based on Weaver Literacy (see Appendix for research) and the Skaneateles Elementary Language Arts Program. Weaver Literacy and the Skaneateles Elementary Language Arts Program began with an educational study trip to New Zealand in 1988. From the knowledge gained in New Zealand, along with research in language arts done in the United States, my colleagues and I developed this unique literacy program. The Skaneateles program has won two International Reading Association Exemplary Reading Awards and the school has achieved the National School of Excellence Award. In 2003, the Skaneateles Central School District received the New York State Governor's Award of Excellence. This award has only been given to four other school districts in New York state since it began over ten years ago.

Many other schools in New York have implemented Weaver Literacy and have had remarkable results. One small city school implemented Weaver Literacy and saw their state scores improve by 20 percent in one year. This book was written to share this program in the hopes that other teachers could realize similar improvements and successes.

How to Use This Book

The format of this book makes it easy to assess students and then provide appropriate intervention instruction. Chapter 4 discusses the factors influencing literacy development at these early ages, drawing on research on how children learn and grow as readers and writers. The major aspects of literacy development are presented within the context of balanced instruction. The instruction that occurs in guided reading, shared reading, read aloud, and the other components of balanced literacy (discussed more fully in Chapter 4) serves as the framework for the assessments.

Chapters 7–9 provide the assessments for each grade level, diagnostic placement tools to begin instruction, clear guidelines on how to administer the assessments and score them using rubrics, and record-keeping forms. The tools provided here enable you to chart scores easily and see individual and whole-class needs at a glance. RTI Benchmark Charts are also included. These charts are linked to the rubric scores and indicate the need to increase intensity or change the method of instruction. There are three assessments per grade level, given at weeks 12, 24, and 36 of the school year (in addition to the baseline) so you have a periodic reading of the whole class' literacy development. Used in conjunction with anecdotal notes and other informal assessments, these assessments provide an invaluable tool for planning and differentiating instruction.

The final section of this book is devoted to intervention instruction for the literacy aspects of print conventions, word recognition, comprehension, and writing, so teachers can immediately translate assessment data into instructional practice. Parent Home Activities are included in the intervention chapters (Chapters 11–14) to assist teachers in involving parents in their children's learning.

I recommend administering the assessments and interventions during the guided reading component of literacy instruction. During this time, you work with small groups of students with similar skill levels and needs. That's not to say it's the only time teaching and assessing can occur; I simply find it the best setting in which to administer the assessments and interventions in this book.

I hope this book serves as a companion in your quest to help all students become successful readers and writers.

Chapter 2

Response to Intervention (RTI): Description, Process, Need for Monitoring Assessment

Response to Intervention, or RTI, may seem like a new concept, but in reality effective teachers have always used this approach in their teaching. That is, when students are taught a specific concept, skill, or strategy, teachers assess whether it has been learned. Based on the assessment results, teachers reteach students who need additional instruction by selecting a different method, material, or technique. If one or more students continue to struggle, the teacher might ask a colleague or reading professional for other ideas. After working with students for a period of time with this alternate instruction, teachers reassess them. Hopefully, students succeed and continue their work in the classroom. Those who require more intensive support after these classroom interventions are referred to outside specialists for more extensive instruction and testing.

The RTI model seeks to formalize this sequence of teach-assess-intervene, and it has gained significance as a result of the Disabilities Education Improvement Act of 2004 (IDEA 2004). This federal regulation concerning the placement of students into special education encourages the development of RTI programs in schools to better evaluate students before identifying them as learning disabled. Prior to this 2004 regulation, students could only be identified as learning disabled if there was a discrepancy between the student's ability and academic progress, which was typically identified after extensive testing by outside specialists, such as the reading teacher and the school psychologist. This new regulation impacts classroom teachers in their daily instruction because it asks them to more formally monitor and document students' progress.

Miller and Giugno (2008) identified some general principles to be considered in developing an RTI program, including monitoring student progress over time, incorporating a variety of research based instructional methods, using collaborative problem solving, encouraging parent involvement, and implementing a school-wide effort.

Furthermore, in some states, such as New York (Letter to Superintendents, April 2008), the development and implementation of RTI programs is being mandated on the school and district levels. Educators support RTI programs because, as Shanahan (2008) states, "It is a particularly effective institutional way to be aggressive about kids' learning." By generalizing and formalizing effective practice into a school-wide program, schools seek to provide the best instruction for every student.

RTI Components

There is no one *correct* structure for RTI programs, but the predominate concept associated with RTI is that the intensity and type of instruction will increase over time for students who continue to struggle. Most structures include at least three tiers (National Joint Commission on Learning Disability, 2005; Shanahan, 2008), spanning regular classroom instruction, targeted interventions, and evaluations for specific learning disabilities. Moving from one tier to another requires the evaluation of a range of assessment data for each student.

The other components of RTI programs include quality instruction, monitoring assessments, collaborative problem-solving teams, and parent involvement. Looking more closely into these components will help the teacher understand the purpose and importance of them in the RTI program.

Multi-tiered Structure

Using tiers in RTI programs is essential for providing the appropriate type and intensity of instruction for in-need students. As Shanahan (2008) explains, most educators agree on the first tier and last tier. The first tier includes all students receiving instruction from the classroom teacher. Students are regularly assessed so teachers can monitor their progress and identify students lagging behind on any given lesson. The classroom teacher reteaches as needed and monitors the learning of all students while continuing to teach the curriculum.

The middle tier—or tiers—involve more intense and differentiated instruction for the students identified as lagging behind their peers. The specific instruction is based on the data provided by the monitoring assessments. These middle tiers may also include supplemental instruction provided by another professional, either in the classroom or in an outside setting. Each student's progress is monitored over a period of time using assessments. Additional staff development or training for the classroom teacher is often a component of Tier 2 interventions.

The reading specialist or literacy coach is instrumental in supporting teachers working in the middle tiers. These professionals have a clear understanding of the developmental continuum of literacy and can share the latest research and insights with classroom teachers. They can offer support in developing reading fluency, vocabulary, and comprehension as well as maintaining motivation in reading (Shanahan, 2008). Support in writing is equally important, and these professionals can offer their expertise in that area as well.

In addition to this knowledge base, reading professionals can provide diagnostic testing, staff development, and/or direct instruction to students. They can also be effective in supervising the reading program.

If students continue to struggle after appropriate classroom interventions, they are moved to the final tier, where they are evaluated for inclusion in special education.

Quality Literacy Instruction

There seems to be a general consensus that students receive quality instruction from effective teachers. It also seems that what teachers do in the classroom—as opposed to their credentials—produces the quality instruction (Williams & Baumann, 2008). From their review of the research, Williams and Baumann (2008) identified some specific characteristics of the effective literacy teacher.

Effective teachers hold high expectations for all students and design instruction so that everyone can succeed. They know that learning is social, and they incorporate activities and techniques such as cooperative learning, discussion groups, literature circles, and so on to capitalize on the social nature of learning.

Effective teachers spend limited time on whole-group instruction; they mostly work with small groups, and they value student independence. They incorporate learning centers, projects, research papers, and independent writing activities into regular classroom work.

Effective teachers use a variety of strategies in their teaching, including direct instruction, modeling, think alouds, demonstrations, and problem-solving tasks. These teachers have in-depth knowledge of numerous methods and techniques and can use them effectively. They easily convert theory into practice in the classroom.

In addition, the effective teacher uses a variety of materials to support these methods and techniques, including different genres of literature, authentic texts, basals, textbooks, magazine articles, Internet content, and other content-area material. They integrate literacy skills and strategies across the content areas.

Effective teachers use multiple assessments to evaluate students' learning and adjust instruction based on the results. These assessments might be formal, performance-based, informal, or diagnostic. Using a variety of assessments provides the teacher with a multi-faceted view of students in terms of learning. Teachers can then differentiate instruction to meet the needs of various learning styles and levels.

Effective teachers find numerous ways to help students connect to content, and they provide support as students learn. They use specific praise and try to motivate them to learn by giving them challenges and goals for learning. They display student work in the classroom to encourage learning and to showcase accomplishments.

Lastly, the personal qualities of an effective teacher include compassion, flexibility, and enthusiasm. Effective teachers empathize with their students and are sensitive to their needs; they adapt instruction as appropriate. They share their own interests with the students and conduct energetic, dynamic lessons.

In summary, here is a chart showing the characteristics of effective teachers or quality instruction in a classroom.

Quality Literacy Teaching

Philosophy of Teaching
- High expectations of students
- Learning is social (e.g., cooperative learning, discussion groups)
- Limited use of whole-group instruction (e.g., small groups for instruction, one to one conferencing)
- Foster independence in students (e.g., learning centers)

Instructional Practices
- Variety of methods/techniques (e.g., direct instruction, modeling, discussion)
- Multiple materials (e.g., literature, basals)
- Small-group instruction emphasis
- Explicit or direct instruction is predominant
- Literacy instruction is integrated in all content areas
- Use of multiple assessments (e.g., formal, informal, diagnostic)

Engaging Students in Learning
- Praises students often
- Motivational or challenge activities
- Students set goals
- Classroom environment supports interactive learning (e.g., centers, projects)
- Displays work of students (e.g., bulletin boards, projects, student writing)

Personal Qualities
- Compassionate with students (e.g., empathy)
- Flexibility (e.g., teaches to needs of students)
- Enthusiasm for learning (e.g., dynamic lessons)

❀ Monitoring Assessments

Assessments are the most critical aspect of any RTI program because they provide specific information about students' progress, which enables teachers to focus their instruction on actual student need. Using a variety of ongoing assessments is critical for establishing a complete picture of students' abilities and needs. For example, if a teacher uses an oral fluency assessment with no comprehension component, then the student may appear to be on level in oral reading even though his or her comprehension is incomplete.

The types of assessments selected need to be balanced among formal, informal, and diagnostic measurements for well-rounded instructional data. The frequency of assessment data needs to be considered as well, such as yearly or quarterly testing. Here is a diagram showing the different types of assessments that might be given in a school for periodic assessment.

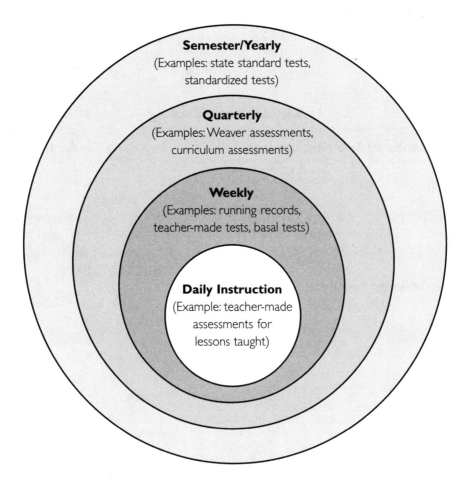

The Weaver assessments in this book are most appropriate for quarterly assessments. However, since they are performance based and diagnostic, you can use them to make informal assessments for daily or weekly instruction.

✴ Collaborative Teams

The purpose of collaborative teams is to establish a formal setting for discussing students' learning and sharing ideas for instruction. Collaborative teams can also provide support for classroom teachers, such as coaching or staff development. Effective teachers have always sought new ways of teaching struggling learners, drawing on the expertise and experience of their colleagues and support professionals such as the reading teacher or literacy coach.

The more formal collaborative or decision-making team can include the classroom teacher, reading professional, special education teacher, principal, speech language professional, and any other teacher involved with assessing students, such as the English Language Learner teacher or social worker. It is also beneficial to have the school psychologist participate. The team can recommend instructional methods or techniques for the classroom teacher to try with a struggling student. Together the team will plan the appropriate instruction for the student and identify necessary assessments to monitor progress.

Some schools have a child-study team or some type of committee that oversees struggling students or classified special education students. This type of school team can become the RTI collaborative team in the program.

In addition, this collaborative team becomes the evaluation team for children who move to the final tier. The team is aware of all the intervention strategies that have been used, have seen the assessments, and now must provide a formal evaluation to determine if specific children have a learning disability. The meetings of this team are documented and provide data for the RTI program.

✴ Parent Involvement

Parent involvement is always important in a school-wide effort. In terms of the RTI perspective, it is suggested that parents are kept informed of their child's progress and also contacted if a formal evaluation becomes necessary.

There can be many forms of parent involvement in a school, from volunteering opportunities in the classroom to curriculum nights to open houses. The classroom teacher can send home monthly calendars summarizing the curriculum for the month as well as classroom activities. Displaying student work on bulletin boards can inform parents of what students are accomplishing in academics.

Parents can also be involved with their children by helping them complete practice activities or projects provided by the classroom teacher at home. At the end of each intervention chapter in this book, I include several home activities for parents to complete with their children. Teachers can suggest these home activities as students are identified as needing more practice in these areas.

Report cards are one of the most common ways teachers inform parents of the progress of their child's learning. However, if the report card just has "Reading B" listed, then the academic progress information is limited. Here are some examples of report card listings that would be more informative to parents on their child's literacy progress.

Kindergarten Example:

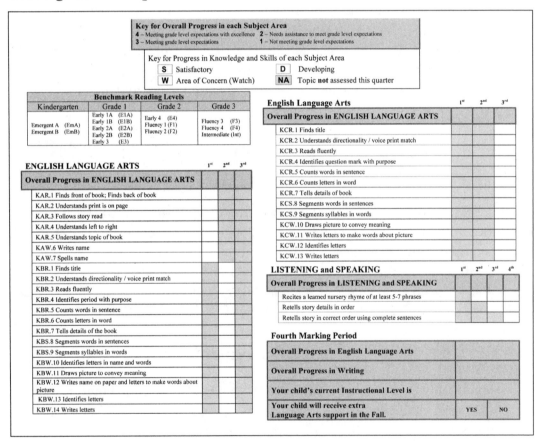

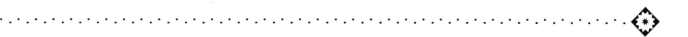

Grade 1 Example:

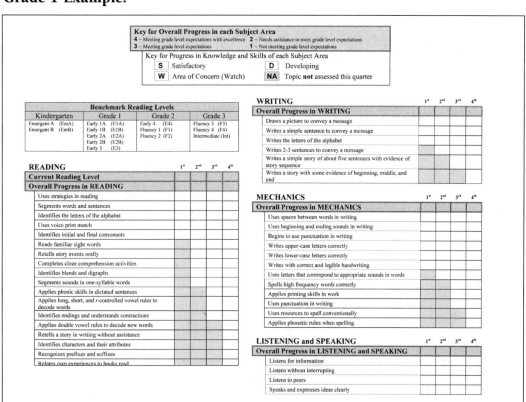

Key for Overall Progress in each Subject Area
4 – Meeting grade level expectations with excellence   2 – Needs assistance to meet grade level expectations
3 – Meeting grade level expectations   1 – Not meeting grade level expectations

Key for Progress in Knowledge and Skills of each Subject Area
| S | Satisfactory | D | Developing |
| W | Area of Concern (Watch) | NA | Topic **not** assessed this quarter |

Benchmark Reading Levels

Kindergarten	Grade 1	Grade 2	Grade 3
Emergent A (EmA)	Early 1A (E1A)	Early 4 (E4)	Fluency 3 (F3)
Emergent B (EmB)	Early 1B (E1B)	Fluency 1 (F1)	Fluency 4 (F4)
	Early 2A (E2A)	Fluency 2 (F2)	Intermediate (Int)
	Early 2B (E2B)		
	Early 3 (E3)		

READING

	1st	2nd	3rd	4th
Current Reading Level				
Overall Progress in READING				
Uses strategies in reading				
Segments words and sentences				
Identifies the letters of the alphabet				
Uses voice print match				
Identifies initial and final consonants				
Reads familiar sight words				
Retells story events orally				
Completes cloze comprehension activities				
Identifies blends and digraphs				
Segments sounds in one-syllable words				
Applies phonic skills in dictated sentences				
Applies long, short, and r-controlled vowel rules to decode words				
Identifies endings and understands contractions				
Applies double vowel rules to decode new words				
Retells a story in writing without assistance				
Identifies characters and their attributes				
Recognizes prefixes and suffixes				
Relates own experiences to books read				

WRITING

	1st	2nd	3rd	4th
Overall Progress in WRITING				
Draws a picture to convey a message				
Writes a simple sentence to convey a message				
Writes the letters of the alphabet				
Writes 2-3 sentences to convey a message				
Writes a simple story of about five sentences with evidence of story sequence				
Writes a story with some evidence of beginning, middle, and end				

MECHANICS

	1st	2nd	3rd	4th
Overall Progress in MECHANICS				
Uses spaces between words in writing				
Uses beginning and ending sounds in writing				
Begins to use punctuation in writing				
Writes upper-case letters correctly				
Writes lower-case letters correctly				
Writes with correct and legible handwriting				
Uses letters that correspond to appropriate sounds in words				
Spells high frequency words correctly				
Applies printing skills in work				
Uses punctuation in writing				
Uses resources to spell conventionally				
Applies phonetic rules when spelling				

LISTENING and SPEAKING

	1st	2nd	3rd	4th
Overall Progress in LISTENING and SPEAKING				
Listens for information				
Listens without interrupting				
Listens to peers				
Speaks and expresses ideas clearly				

Grade 2 Example:

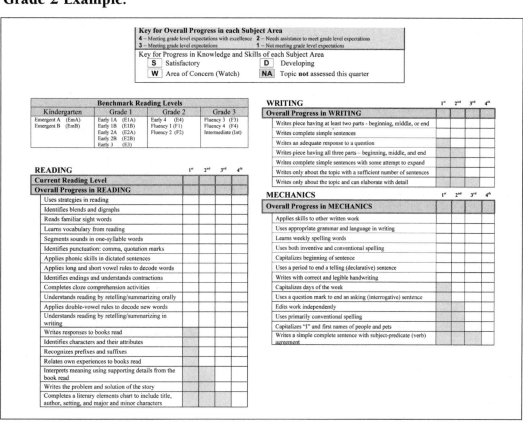

Key for Overall Progress in each Subject Area
4 – Meeting grade level expectations with excellence   2 – Needs assistance to meet grade level expectations
3 – Meeting grade level expectations   1 – Not meeting grade level expectations

Key for Progress in Knowledge and Skills of each Subject Area
| S | Satisfactory | D | Developing |
| W | Area of Concern (Watch) | NA | Topic **not** assessed this quarter |

Benchmark Reading Levels

Kindergarten	Grade 1	Grade 2	Grade 3
Emergent A (EmA)	Early 1A (E1A)	Early 4 (E4)	Fluency 3 (F3)
Emergent B (EmB)	Early 1B (E1B)	Fluency 1 (F1)	Fluency 4 (F4)
	Early 2A (E2A)	Fluency 2 (F2)	Intermediate (Int)
	Early 2B (E2B)		
	Early 3 (E3)		

READING

	1st	2nd	3rd	4th
Current Reading Level				
Overall Progress in READING				
Uses strategies in reading				
Identifies blends and digraphs				
Reads familiar sight words				
Learns vocabulary from reading				
Segments sounds in one-syllable words				
Identifies punctuation: comma, quotation marks				
Applies phonic skills in dictated sentences				
Applies long and short vowel rules to decode words				
Identifies endings and understands contractions				
Completes cloze comprehension activities				
Understands reading by retelling/summarizing orally				
Applies double-vowel rules to decode new words				
Understands reading by retelling/summarizing in writing				
Writes responses to books read				
Identifies characters and their attributes				
Recognizes prefixes and suffixes				
Relates own experiences to books read				
Interprets meaning using supporting details from the book read				
Writes the problem and solution of the story				
Completes a literary elements chart to include title, author, setting, and major and minor characters				

WRITING

	1st	2nd	3rd	4th
Overall Progress in WRITING				
Writes piece having at least two parts - beginning, middle, or end				
Writes complete simple sentences				
Writes an adequate response to a question				
Writes piece having all three parts – beginning, middle, and end				
Writes complete simple sentences with some attempt to expand				
Writes only about the topic with a sufficient number of sentences				
Writes only about the topic and can elaborate with detail				

MECHANICS

	1st	2nd	3rd	4th
Overall Progress in MECHANICS				
Applies skills to other written work				
Uses appropriate grammar and language in writing				
Learns weekly spelling words				
Uses both inventive and conventional spelling				
Capitalizes beginning of sentence				
Uses a period to end a telling (declarative) sentence				
Writes with correct and legible handwriting				
Capitalizes days of the week				
Uses a question mark to end an asking (interrogative) sentence				
Edits work independently				
Uses primarily conventional spelling				
Capitalizes "I" and first names of people and pets				
Writes a simple complete sentence with subject-predicate (verb) agreement				

School RTI Program Development

Implementing a school-wide program takes place over time. The first step is to identify what RTI components are already in place, and then note which components are in need of partial development and total development. Lastly, an action plan with time lines and people responsible for the tasks should be created. Available resources are critical to its timely completion. The following chart can assist in the implementation plan.

RTI Component	Characteristics Present in School	Modifications or Additions Needed	Time Line for Completion
Tier 1: Classroom Program • Curriculum • Assessments • Staff Development			
Middle Tier(s): Interventions • Support Personnel • Additional Instruction for Students • Staff Development Training • Assessments			
Last Tier: Formal Evaluation • Written Process for Evaluation • Data Collection Forms • Personnel for Evaluation • Process for Notification of Parents			
Quality of Instruction Characteristics What area do teachers need more staff development or training? • Philosophy • Instructional Practices • Engaging Students • Personal Qualities			
Monitoring Assessments • Formal • Informal • Diagnostic • Yearly • Quarterly • Weekly • Daily			
Collaborative Team • Problem-Solving Groups • Personnel			
Parent Involvement • Classroom Activities • Projects • Home Activities • Report Cards (Parent Friendly)			

In summary, while the concept of RTI is not necessarily new to teaching, the formalization of the concept is significant. Classroom teachers require information on the concept so they can be more effective in their teaching and to help realize the goal of quality instruction for all students.

Balancing Appropriate Curriculum, State Standards, and State Assessments for Effective Literacy Instruction

In an educational climate dominated by federal regulations, state standards, and state assessments, teachers have experienced increasing pressure and anxiety for students to perform well on state assessments. Add to that the requirements of an RTI program, and teachers can be easily overwhelmed. However, as discussed in the previous chapter, the foundation of RTI is good teaching informed by regular assessments of student progress. An RTI program simply formalizes this best practice. Federal and state requirements seek to do the same, and if all these components are integrated, the result is a comprehensive, developmentally appropriate curriculum delivered in ways that meet the needs of students. This chapter offers guidelines to help you focus your instruction for optimum effectiveness while meeting all mandated requirements.

Literacy Curriculum

In many schools, the basal reader being used in the district determines the language arts or literacy curriculum. For others, there is a limited curriculum and teachers have the responsibility for fleshing it out. Basal readers or core reading programs of today are comprehensive and provide numerous support materials. However, the management and use of all these materials can be frustrating, especially for inexperienced teachers. Basal readers or the core reading program usually have so many activities and suggestions that teachers, knowing they can not include all of this material in their teaching, are frustrated by what to choose for instruction. They are fearful that if something is left out, it may be critical. The basal publishers are not clear as to what is important and what is less important. This book guides the teacher's instruction through the use of the Weaver assessments. Likewise, teachers who are using a workshop model of instruction will find the Weaver assessments especially useful for guidance in their instruction. The following section provides teachers with a framework for a balanced literacy curriculum and discusses continuums of learning for the various aspects of such a curriculum. The Weaver assessments in this book evaluate the critical elements of reading and writing from the curriculum at grades K–2.

A balanced curriculum includes a developmental continuum of concepts and skills across the grade levels in the areas of reading, writing, listening, and speaking. All four of these areas are interrelated in terms of learning. A child's listening skills are directly related to speaking, and so on. Figure 3.1 illustrates the importance of teaching the language arts with an integrated approach because the learning in one area impacts the learning in other areas.

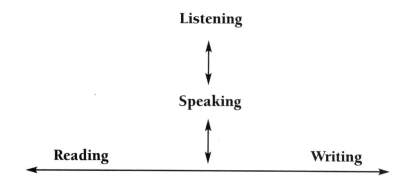

3.1 Relationship of Reading, Writing, Listening, and Speaking

In every district's curriculum document, each of the four literacy areas—reading, writing, listening, and speaking—needs to be broken down into a discrete set of grade-appropriate skills correlated to the materials available in the schools, such as the basals, leveled readers, and classroom libraries. The placement of these skills and state standards objectives can be driven by the timetable of the basal company and when the state assessments are administered. Having this overall plan, and incorporating systematic monitoring of student learning through assessments such as those included in this book, enables teachers to track student progress and provide additional instruction based on students' needs. Assessment helps teachers decide when they need to reteach concepts and skills before continuing with the curriculum. Ongoing monitoring also informs teachers which students already grasp the concepts and can advance more quickly or be instructed at a higher level of complexity. RTI programs function using this same concept, and having a balanced curriculum is essential as the first step for instruction. Here is an example of a K–2 developmental, basic curriculum without references to a basal or any state standards. The Weaver assessments in this book follow this general curriculum and can be adapted for use with any curriculum.

Kindergarten Curriculum Example

Quarter	Elements	Materials or Basal Reference	State Standards	Assessments
1	**Listening/Speaking** • Listens to stories and can express the main idea • Expresses the main idea of the story in complete sentences **Reading** • Points to title • Understands print is on page • Knows reading goes from left to right • Follows a story read aloud using print • Identifies 26/55 letters • Identifies name from other print • Writes 8 letters **Writing** • Writes name • Identifies letters in name in print • Draws pictures to convey a message • Writes letters to make words			Weaver Kindergarten Diagnostic Assessment
2	**Listening/Speaking** • Listens to stories and can relate several details • Relates details of story in complete sentences • Recites a learned nursery rhyme of at least 5 to 7 phrases **Reading** • Points to title • Understands directionality and attempts return sweep • Follows print when read to • Reads early emergent book successfully • Identifies period and gives purpose • Identifies concrete and high-frequency words • Counts words in sentences • Counts letters in words • Segments words in sentences • Segments syllables in words • Identifies 40/54 letters • Writes 15/52 letters **Writing** • Writes name with appropriate upper- and lowercase letters on a line • Identifies letters in name and other words • Draws picture to convey meaning • Writes letters to make words within lines			Weaver Kindergarten 12 Week Assessment

Quarter	Elements	Materials or Basal Reference	State Standards	Assessments
3	**Listening/Speaking** • Listens to stories and can relate beginning, middle, and end of story • Relates story in complete sentences **Reading** • Points to title • Understands directionality and return sweep • Voice-print matches • Reads emergent book successfully • Identifies question mark and gives purpose • Identifies concrete and high-frequency words • Counts words in sentences • Counts letters in words • Segments words in sentences • Segments syllables in words • Identifies 40/55 letters • Writes 20/52 letters **Writing** • Writes name with appropriate upper- and lowercase letters on a line • Draws picture to convey meaning • Writes letters to make words within lines			Weaver Kindergarten 24 Week Assessment
4	**Listening/Speaking** • Listens to stories and can relate beginning, middle, and end of story • Relates own story in complete sentences with beginning, middle, and end **Reading** • Basic print conventions used • Reads late emergent book successfully • Identifies punctuation • Identifies concrete and high-frequency words • Segments words in sentences • Segments syllables in words • Identifies sounds of several letters • Identifies 52/55 letters • Writes 35/52 letters **Writing** • Writes letters to make words for a story • Writes words to make simple sentences			Weaver Kindergarten 36 Week Assessment

First Grade Curriculum Example

Quarter	Elements	Materials or Basal Reference	State Standards	Assessments
1	**Listening/Speaking** • Listens to stories and responds to questions • Listens to teacher directions and is able to carry out directions • Tells a story with a beginning, middle, and end • Able to converse with a peer or adult in clear, full sentences **Reading** • Review left to right and return sweep, punctuation (period, question mark, exclamation point), capital letters at beginning of sentence, for names • Introduce comma, quotation marks, word differences • Review kindergarten vocabulary • Review initial and final consonants • Review alphabet • Review use of picture in reading text • Review use of initial sounds in reading text • Introduce story vocabulary, blends and digraphs, word families (break and make) • Introduce using structure to help decode words • Review story line and sequence of story • Review days of week, number words, colors, months • Read fantasy stories, folktales to identify story line of beginning, middle, end • Teach concept of fiction **Writing** • Review writing of alphabet and a simple sentence • Writes 3–4 simple sentences in story format • Writes dictation sentences using word families			Weaver Kindergarten 36 Week Assessment
2	**Listening/Speaking** • Listens to stories and responds to questions • Listens to teacher directions and is able to carry out directions • Tells a story with a beginning, middle, and end • Able to converse with a peer or adult in clear, full sentences **Reading** • Introduce nonfiction text format—pictures/captions, index, table of contents, glossary • Review all punctuation marks, use in writing, italic and bold meaning and use • Introduce story vocabulary, short, long, r-controlled vowels, word families (break and make), using meaning first to help decode words then looking for patterns, compound words, endings of words • Introduce concept of nonfiction, introduce facts • Instruct fiction: literary elements of title, author, setting, oral summary **Writing** • Writes 3–4 simple sentences in informational, descriptive format, dictation sentences using word families with vowel patterns • Writes author, title, setting of books • Writes stories of minimum of 5 sentences in length, dictation for punctuation, capitalization use			Weaver Grade 1 12 Week Assessment

Quarter	Elements	Materials or Basal Reference	State Standards	Assessments
3	**Listening/Speaking** • Listens to stories and responds to questions • Listens to teacher directions and is able to carry out directions • Tells a story with a beginning, middle, and end • Begins to make class presentations **Reading** • Review all punctuation marks, use in writing, introduce paragraphing indentation and quotation marks • Introduce story vocabulary, double vowels and patterns by using meaning first to help decode words then looking for patterns • Review contractions, endings of words, and compounds • Instruct fiction: literary elements of title, author, setting, written summary, introduce climax, character attributes • Instruct nonfiction: review facts and information text **Writing** • Writes author, title, setting, summary of books • Writes stories of minimum of 7 sentences in length using adjectives to elaborate • Uses dictation for punctuation, capitalization use • Writes short informational pieces with minimum of 3 facts • Instruct conventional spelling practice			Weaver Grade 1 24 Week Assessment
4	**Listening/Speaking** • Listens to stories and responds to questions • Listens to teacher directions and is able to carry out directions • Tells a story with a beginning, middle, and end • Begins to make class presentations **Reading** • Review all punctuation marks and use in writing • Introduce paragraphing indentation and quotation writing • Introduce story vocabulary, double vowels and vowel patterns, using meaning first to help decode words then looking for patterns • Review contractions, endings of words, and compounds • Instruct prefixes and suffixes • Instruct fiction: literary elements of title, author, setting, written summary, climax, character attributes, problem/resolution • Instruct nonfiction: review facts and information text **Writing** • Writes author, title, setting, summary, problem/resolution, character attributes of books • Writes stories of minimum of 7–10 sentences in length using adjectives and more complex sentence structure • Uses dictation for punctuation, capitalization instruction • Writes short informational pieces with minimum of 3 facts • Practices conventional spelling • Introduce writing answers to questions			Weaver Grade 1 36 Week Assessment

Second Grade Curriculum Example

Quarter	Elements	Materials or Basal Reference	State Standards	Assessments
1	**Listening/Speaking** • Understands the main idea of nonfiction text from listening to text • Identifies a fact from listening to nonfiction text • Can explain learning to class and formulate questions about learning **Reading** • Refines the use of the sound/symbol strategy in decoding (double vowels and phonetic clusters) • Develops vocabulary using affixes and roots (meaning focus) • Understands the details of nonfiction text • Acquires new vocabulary through use of context clues • Understands the meaning of affixes and roots • Understands the information in nonfiction text by written response • Identifies the facts in nonfiction text • Understands the comprehension pattern of compare/contrast • Understands how a Venn diagram is a graphic organizer for the pattern of compare/contrast • Reviews literal meaning of sentences • Reviews making predictions about a text • Instruct in locating table of contents, glossary, and index **Writing** • Understands how to write a complete sentence • Recognizes a sentence • Understands difference between statement and question • Understands how to use facts in writing • Understands how to write a response using the question as a stem • Identifies paragraphs in text and understands their use • Can write a piece using given facts			Weaver Grade 1 36 Week Assessment
2	**Listening/Speaking** • Understands the events in a tale • Responds in writing to comprehension questions about the story • Makes presentations to the class • Participates in discussion in class **Reading** • Refines the use of the sound/symbol strategy in decoding (double vowels and phonetic clusters) • Develops vocabulary using affixes and roots (meaning focus) • Uses cueing strategies during silent reading • Understands synonyms, antonyms, and homophones • Identifies character attributes • Identifies main idea of selection • Identifies supporting details • Recalls sequence of events or ideas • Can alphabetize to the 2nd letter • Follows written directions • Learns dictionary skills • Understands the literary elements associated with fairy tales (characters, attributes, problem, resolution, summary) • Understands the differences and similarities in other versions of the fairy tales • Understands the meaning of the symbols, inferences, etc. in the fairy tales • Understands the comprehension pattern of compare/contrast			Weaver Grade 2 12 Week Assessment

Quarter	Elements	Materials or Basal Reference	State Standards	Assessments
2 cont.	**Writing** • Understands how to write a complete sentence • Understands how to put given story events into a logical order of the story • Understands how to write a response using the question as a stem • Can write a piece that includes a problem and resolution • Uses simple statements to respond to comprehension questions • Creates a written summary for text read • Creates a topic sentence and expands on the topic with sentences that result in a beginning, middle, and end • Differentiates between sentence fragments, complete sentences, and run-ons • Uses commas to separate items in a series, with noun of direct address (i.e., Sue, go home.) in dates and places • Recognizes and uses adjectives • Recognizes dialogue—quotation marks • Identifies exclamatory sentences • Distinguishes between asking and telling statements			
3	**Listening/Speaking** • Listens for understanding • Listens for connections • Writes responses • Makes presentations to the class • Participates in discussion in class **Reading** • Finds and uses clues to solve mystery • Understands problem/resolution • Understands and applies compound words, contractions, plurals, affixes • Makes inferences • Introduce making judgments about a selection • Introduce author's point of view • Introduce drawing conclusions • Introduce cause and effect • Introduce figurative language and humor in text • Introduce different literary forms (folk tale, historical fiction, biographies) **Writing** • Writes using problem/resolution pattern • Writes responses • Uses descriptive language • Combines simple sentences to form compound sentences • Expands writing through use of adjectives or describing words • Writes reading responses that show interpretation of text • Writes a friendly letter using proper format and punctuation • Understands and expands sentences in writing • Begins to write in paragraphs • Writes from personal experience • Edits for mechanics • Recognizes and uses both adjectives and adverbs • Begins to use quotation marks • Begins to use the apostrophe to show ownership or in a contraction • Uses conventional spelling primarily			Weaver Grade 2 24 Week Assessment

Quarter	Elements	Materials or Basal Reference	State Standards	Assessments
4	**Listening/Speaking** • Listens for understanding of poems • Listens for connections/interpretations in poems • Understands the main idea of the poem • Listens for alliteration, rhyming, similes, and metaphors • Responds in writing to the poem **Reading** • Reads for meaning and to appreciate poetry • Understands poetic elements of alliteration and rhyming • Infers from poem • Compares/contrasts poems • Identifies similes and metaphors • Identifies nouns, adjectives, and verbs • Understands synonyms, antonyms, and rhyming words • Applies cueing strategies during silent reading • Understands how to read a poem using punctuation and expression • Reviews dictionary skills **Writing** • Writes using a variety of sentence structures • Writes about topic with supporting details • Writes responses • Uses descriptive language in writing • Uses adjectives and verbs in writing for description • Writes a descriptive paragraph from a picture prompt • Understands and writes diamante and cinquain poems • Uses thesaurus for finding additional words			Weaver Grade 2 36 Week Assessment

In the above comprehensive, developmental curriculum charts, all that is needed is to add your state standards at each grade level to ensure and document that they are being addressed. Likewise, record your basal core reading program and classroom materials. If scope and sequence skills, strategies, and concepts are missing, add them. For instance, if you teach poetry elements in second grade, then those poetry elements need to be included in the curriculum document. The importance of this documentation is to ensure that you are teaching from a balanced, comprehensive curriculum, which includes state standards and required teaching materials.

These curriculum examples demonstrate how over the course of a year a developmental, appropriate literacy curriculum can be divided into school year quarters. Dividing it this way also suggests natural pausing points for assessment. Monitoring student learning as instruction progresses through the school year is essential, and this book gives you the appropriate assessment times and what the expectations or

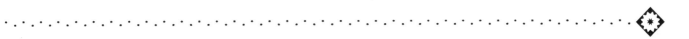

criteria are for each time of the year. You want to expect the appropriate level of learning without frustrating students with inappropriate assessment/learning criteria for their grade level. If students do not meet these expectations, then it's time to move into Tier 2 territory; you'll find research-based intervention strategies and activities in the second half of this book. These are useful for giving individuals or small groups of students extra practice in areas where they need it.

In Chapters 7–9, the specifics of literacy expectations in print conventions, word recognition, comprehension, and writing are mapped out with assessments that evaluate learning in each of these areas. Curriculum, instructional expectations, and assessments all work together to provide cohesive, effective instruction.

☀ State Standards

As a result of NCLB most state education departments have developed state standards. Some states generalize literacy objectives, such as New York, while other states are more specific and detailed, such as Florida. Regardless of the state standards structure, it is important to match them to your curriculum. Doing so documents how you address the state standards and provides an easy format for making sure you cover them.

Some state standards documents include curriculum guides, activities, benchmarks, performance indicators, and teaching ideas. While these extra materials can be helpful in some respects, they can also be confusing for instruction. It seems to work best to have the curriculum developed first and then reference these other materials in the curriculum to enhance the teaching of specific units.

Moreover, some basal core reading publishers will provide basal texts with this cross match between basal lessons and state standards specific to your state. However, the teacher will need to cross check the program standards listed to ensure that all state standards are included. Some programs have less of an emphasis on writing or listening, and you'll be able to address that when you see what's lacking in the program.

In summary, documenting state standards in the curriculum document ensures that instruction is focused on all state standards and provides teachers with an inclusive instructional program.

☀ State Assessments

Most states have developed language arts assessments. Some states test at every grade level, while others only test certain subjects at certain grade levels. The final piece to a balanced, appropriate literacy curriculum is the inclusion of the format, methodology, and techniques used in these state assessments. In order to include these aspects, it is beneficial to analyze the state exam to determine where the instructional focus should lie. State tests are mandated, so it is important to familiarize students with their format and to offer them instruction and practice with the types of questions and tasks used on the tests. Some school districts require students to take district-developed assessments while others require the basal tests to be administered; in any case, students should receive instruction in how to tackle the tests.

To gather data about the nature of an assessment, use the following procedure to determine the readability of passages, the types of questions asked, and the degree of difficulty of the questions. For writing assessments, determine the type of writing prompt and how mechanics are assessed using the Writing Tests Procedure outlined below.

Reading Tests Procedure

1. Type or copy a sample passage from a past assessment into a word processing program that includes a readability formula. (For example, Microsoft Word uses the Flesch-Kincaid Readability Formula.) Note the readability level.

2. Read the passage and answer the questions, noting whether the answers were stated in the passage (explicit) or the student needed to draw conclusions or infer from the passage (implicit).

3. Determine the type of each question. Figure 3.2 lists the most common types of multiple choice questions along with explanations of them.

4. Tally the different types of questions and the number of implicit/explicit questions. Calculate the percentage of these items per passage and then per test.

5. From the data gathered, determine what types of questions require more instruction. For example, if 80 percent of the questions were main idea questions, you would want to provide extra practice in this area.

Writing Tests Procedures

1. For a past assessment, determine the type of prompt presented. (See Figure 3.3 for common prompt types.)

2. If more than one prompt is given, tally the types presented or use back issues of the writing tests to get more examples.

3. Include these types of prompts in your curriculum.

4. If mechanics examples are presented, note the format and include them in the curriculum.

Most Common Multiple Choice Questions	
Finding the Main Idea (*Summarizing*) (MI)	What was the whole piece about: Summarize it.
Recalling Facts and Details (*Skim, Scan, Text Pattern*) (FD)	Skim and scan the text to find the specific event or phrase. Read that section carefully to find the detail.
Understanding Sequence (*Text Pattern*) (Seq)	Look for the signal words that give the sequence (first, second, next, then, finally, etc.).
Recognizing Cause and Effect (*Text Pattern*) (CE)	What happened? (effect) What caused it to happen? What are the reasons? Why questions are always CE.
Comparing and Contrasting (*Text Pattern*) (CC)	Look for two topics being discussed. How are they the same and how are they different?
Making Predictions (*Previewing*) (Pred)	Using the title, pictures, graphics, and subheadings, try to decide what would happen next or another resolution to the problem.
Finding Word Meanings in Context (*Vocabulary Development*) (WM)	What do the other words in the sentence help me to understand about the word (noun, verb, etc.)? What do the other sentences tell us about this word?
Drawing Conclusions and Making Inferences (*Evaluating*) (DC)	Think about the text read. What is it similar to that you have already read or know about? Using what you know from life experiences, what is your best conclusion?
Distinguishing Between Fact and Opinion (*Genre Elements*) (FO)	Look for names, dates, numbers for facts, "Can be proven" statements. If phrase or statement has feelings, beliefs, descriptive adjectives like great, good, fine, poor, then it is probably an opinion.
Identifying Author's Purpose (*Theme, Evaluating*) (AP)	What did you learn from the text? What are some possible reasons the author wrote this text?
Interpreting Figurative Language (*Vocabulary Development*) (FL)	What images does the language bring to mind that are imaginary to the text topic or character?
Distinguishing between Real and Make-Believe (*Genre Elements*) (RM)	What genre is the text? Why do you believe it is that genre?
Identifying Problem/Resolution (*Text Pattern*) (PR)	What was the problem in the text? What are the steps taken to resolve the problem? The resolution is:
Text Patterns (TP)	What type of story is this passage? (mystery)

Figure 3.2

Writing Prompts	
Type of Writing Prompt	**Aspects of Instruction**
Narrative	**Story** • Written with beginning, middle, end • Includes characters • Has a plot, probably a problem/resolution • Includes feelings, emotions **Personal Narrative** • Written with beginning, middle, end • Includes characters • Uses personal information and events • Includes feelings, emotions
Expository Essay	**Explain** • Includes facts, reasons, examples • Organized in order of importance, cause-effect, comparison **How-to (Procedure)** • Steps of procedure • Organized in time order **Persuade** • Choose a topic that can be argued • Write the statement of argument • Present both sides with evidence • Use facts, not opinions • Organize your arguments

Figure 3.3

The following is an example of one reading passage and how it is analyzed with this procedure (FCAT [Florida Comprehensive Assessment Test] Grade 3, 2006).

Passage 1 on Ladybirds			
Question	**Type of Question** (Using Diag. 3.2)	**Implicit/Explicit**	**State Standard**
1	CE	Implicit	LA.E.2.2.1
2	AP	Implicit	LA. A.2.2.2
3	CE	Implicit	LA.A.2.2.1
4	CE	Implicit	LA.A.2.2.1
5	CE	Explicit	LA.A.2.2.1
6	DC	Implicit	LA.A.2.2.8
7	MI	Implicit	LA.A.2.2.1
8	DC	Implicit	LA.E.1.2.3

Summary of Passage: 88 percent of questions are implicit and 12 percent of the questions are explicit; 50 percent of the questions are cause-effect; 12.5 percent of the questions are author's purpose and main idea; drawing conclusion questions are 25 percent.

In summary, starting with a basic developmental curriculum, inserting the state standards, and analyzing state assessment information will support your instruction and help you focus it. The next chapters offer diagnostic curriculum assessments that can be used for year-long monitoring of students' learning and progress.

Factors Influencing Literacy Development

In a perfect world, teachers would teach reading and writing to children, and they would learn easily. However, we all live in the real world, where factors beyond our control often impede the development of literacy. Children do not understand why learning is so difficult, but it often is. As teachers, we become frustrated and over-whelmed when our instruction is not successful. This chapter provides some insights into

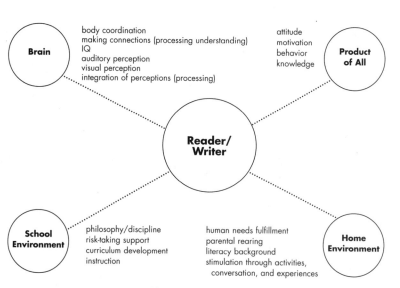

Figure 4.1

factors that can significantly influence literacy development: brain function, home environment, and school setting (see Figure 4.1). Subsequent chapters provide intervention strategies and activities that can help mitigate the effect of any negative factors and build upon the strengths of positive factors.

Brain Functions

The brain is the most amazing organ in the human body. It gives us the life and breath of our being. The numerous ways in which a brain functions, or the processing rate, can affect literacy development. Some of what we know about brain research tells us that the brain can change physiologically as a result of environmental experiences, that certain periods of time in brain growth influence our acquisition of abilities, and that IQ is not necessarily fixed at birth (Wolfe, Brandt, 1998).

Wolfe (2001) describes the functioning of the brain in this way. The senses are receptors that receive data from the outside world. Using working memory, the brain interprets the sensory information, separating important details from insignificant ones and transferring important data to long-term memory. Trying to get learning into long-term memory is the goal of educators. Wolfe explains that novelty, intensity, and movement can increase the attention of the brain, although meaning and emotion seem to be the controllers of what data makes it into long-term memory. Understanding and using these concepts will help educators design more effective instruction to fit the needs and strengths of their students.

Furthermore, the brain develops lasting connections through concrete experiences, representational or symbolic learning, and abstract learning (Wolfe, 2001). Lasting connections comprise the long-term memory of the brain. The more connections we have, the more we have learned. A variety of real-life or concrete experiences should be encouraged for children at all ages, especially the early years of birth to age five, to build their background knowledge. Representational or symbolic learning means using pictures or graphics in addition to letters (reading/writing) and numbers (math) to convey concepts. Having a rich store of experiences to draw on makes it easier to learn from pictures, graphics, and symbols. Abstract learning is conceptual understanding, such as understanding democracy or evaporation. The development of abstract learning requires the use of a higher level of thinking skills. Abstract learning usually is most difficult for the young child. Through direct instruction using concrete experiences and some representational or symbolic experiences, children can acquire this higher level of conceptual understanding. Therefore, designing instruction using concrete examples, graphic organizers, and higher-level thinking skills will help increase the likelihood of long-term learning.

Gardner's multiple intelligences (1983, 1993) describe how multifaceted intelligence can be. He discusses eight types of intelligences that he researched: linguistic, bodily-kinesthetic, spatial, musical, logical-mathematical, intrapersonal, interpersonal, and naturalist. Many of our students have strengths in one or more intelligences rather than a balance among them all. Our awareness of these various intelligences can influence our instruction; we can develop lessons and activities that appeal to various learning styles to build on the strengths of our students. Understanding these various intelligences and capitalizing on students' strengths in these areas will enhance and perhaps increase the connections made by students, which ultimately increases learning.

Wolfe suggests ways to influence learning that harness the brain's power and increase the likelihood that information will make its way to a student's long-term memory. Some of the most effective ways to learn are through real-life problem solving, projects, simulations, role-playing, music, songs, rhymes, chants, writing, hands-on activities, and active rehearsal strategies such as peer teaching.

Instruction should engage the learner in meaningful experiences. Gardner suggests that teachers who use these approaches—which appeal to the various intelligences and incorporate concrete, representational, and abstract experiences—may increase the students' learning rate. The assessments and interventions described in subsequent chapters utilize these powerful influences on learning.

Home Environment

In addition to the physical makeup of an individual's brain, we must consider a student's home environment. Just as every brain functions a bit differently, so does every family. We can use our understanding of a student's home environment to inform our literacy instruction. The ideal home is warm, loving, and responsive, a place where parents, caregivers, and children join together in challenging, fun activities—including literacy activities such as reading aloud—and participate in various activities outside the home, such as trips to the library, zoo, and grocery store. In this environment, children develop close relationships with important adults in their lives and feel safe and supported, empowered to try new things and take risks. Unfortunately, not all students have the benefit of such an ideal background; we must accept this situation and seek ways to engage students and their families in productive literacy experiences at home to foster their overall literacy development.

You can enhance the home-school connection by providing literacy nights for parents, where parents learn how to develop literacy skills in the home setting. You can also hold read-a-thons, where children read at home or parents read to them to see how many books can be read in a time period. Some schools have literacy centers or parent libraries for parents to take out books to share with their children. In addition, parents and caregivers—who universally want to see their children succeed in school—can participate in some of the practice activities included later in this book to help reinforce their child's literacy skills at home.

School Setting

Schools should embrace their students and make the school setting the most conducive it can be to meet the learning needs of its population. Ideally, the school should function as a collaborative system that focuses on helping all children learn to read and write. A child study team is essential to problem-solve ways to assist individual children as they develop literacy, especially when they are identified as having difficulty. Comprehensive diagnostic assessments must be a focus for this team, which might include a school psychologist, speech therapist, reading specialist, special education teacher, and the principal. Extra support in terms of additional instruction is often necessary for children who have difficulty learning to read and write in the typical classroom setting. Reading teachers are a real asset in supporting classroom reading instruction.

In the classroom, you should strive to provide instruction that engages learners, is challenging, has a feedback device, uses a multi-sensory approach, and focuses on students' needs and strengths. Collaborating with other teachers and administrators makes designing a dynamic curriculum exciting and professionally stimulating.

In terms of literacy instruction, you must have a well-rounded and balanced approach to teaching language arts, as described by Mooney (1990). In order to maintain this balance, Weaver (2000) suggests that six teaching components be utilized each day; see the chart below for details.

Read Aloud

Purpose:	To model reading skills and strategies; to introduce or reinforce concepts or content
Instruction:	Read-aloud sessions are approximately 10 to 15 minutes in length and occur daily. In kindergarten, read aloud often occurs twice daily.
Materials:	Classroom library books, library books
Evaluation:	Listening assessments where appropriate. In grades K–2, these listening assessments are often oral discussions about the text read. Depending on the genre read, you might ask questions about the literary elements of the text or about some of the nonfiction concepts or facts.

Shared Reading and Shared Writing

Purpose:	To instruct the whole class in grade-level curriculum; to practice reading and writing strategies with teacher support
Instruction:	I recommend planning shared reading and shared writing together because they both focus on the grade-level curriculum. These instructional sessions are approximately 20 to 40 minutes in length and occur every day. For kindergarten and grade 1, the sessions are usually closer to 20 minutes. Teachers also tend to focus on one activity, shared reading or shared writing, during one session. Often this instructional setting is content related, and may include instruction in spelling and writing mechanics.
Materials:	Shared reading books or classroom books that are on the average reading level for the class
Evaluation:	Quarterly or unit performance assessments. These assessments can be teacher-developed or specific to a publisher.

Guided Reading

Purpose:	To directly instruct students in reading and writing at their instructional level
Instruction:	Guided reading is small-group instruction of not more than eight students. In most classrooms, it takes place every day and is a priority over all other components. To manage a number of groups, teachers rotate them, meeting with three or four groups per day. Group instruction is 15 to 20 minutes long (up to 15 minutes for kindergarten, and up to 20 minutes for grades 1 and 2). In kindergarten, the guided reading groups often focus on language development and readiness skills and are part of learning centers that rotate every 15 minutes. Groups are predominately determined by ability and are evaluated at least every six weeks and adjusted as necessary.
Materials:	Leveled books
Evaluation:	Periodic assessments determine movement in levels and among groups. These assessments can be running records, observations, published assessments, or teacher-developed assessments. This book provides specific assessments for grades K–2. (See chapters 7–9 for grade-level assessments.)

Independent Reading and Independent Writing

Purpose:	To allow children to read and write independently without teacher support, practicing and applying the skills and strategies they've been taught in other settings
Instruction:	Independent reading often involves response journals or some other type of response. Independent writing consists of writing folders with drafts and finished work and/or journals. Independent reading and writing are often scheduled during guided reading time; while the teacher meets with small groups, the rest of the class is reading and writing independently, practicing and applying their literacy skills.
Materials:	Students select their own books and writing topics.
Evaluation:	Teacher-student conferences

Overall Impact

Students' brain function, home environment, and school setting can affect their attitudes and motivation. Attitude can influence how children approach the business of learning to read and write. Motivation is also critical, determining how long children will pursue literacy tasks and what kind of risk-takers they will become. Learning to read and write is a process that requires perseverance and focus. It also requires that children be willing to take risks, to be wrong, and to be problem solvers. School, home, and brain function together affect how children approach the literacy-learning process. As teachers, we can build upon students' innate strengths through a structured, engaging, and balanced literacy program. This book provides tools to identify students' strengths and needs and work with them within the balanced reading framework.

Aspects of Literacy
Instruction in K–2

Guided reading is where differentiated, direct instruction of reading takes place. Teachers gather small groups of children who are working through similar challenges in reading and provide explicit teaching and support. In Fountas and Pinnell's words, "It is through guided reading . . . that teachers can show children how to read and can support children as they read" (1996, p. 1). Guided reading, then, is the ideal place to instruct students in each of the four key literacy areas: print conventions, word recognition, comprehension, and writing. This chapter discusses each of these four areas in depth and lays out expectations for students in grades K, 1, and 2 for each of the areas. The assessments and interventions presented later in this book are based on these understandings of literacy.

Understandings of Overall Literacy Development

Our understanding of literacy learning has undergone many changes since the 1960s (Pearson & Stephens, 1994). The focus then was on the coding system of our language. Teachers felt that the primary purpose of literacy instruction was to teach the alphabet and letter-sound correspondence. Therefore, phonics and skills instruction formed the basis of the curriculum. During this time, researchers from several academic disciplines began studying literacy, each from their own discipline's perspective. Synthesizing the work done by many different fields over the past several decades has helped researchers develop a greater understanding of literacy development and effective teaching practices.

From the linguists, psycholinguists, cognitive psychologists, and sociolinguists, we have established new understandings of literacy, as summarized by Pearson and Stephens (1994):

◆ Children come to school with the ability to construct language.

◆ Children can more easily relate to reading material that is close to their speaking language and, therefore, learn from it.

◆ Language has a surface structure and a deep structure; reading material which enhances the reader's understanding of the deep structure is easier to read.

◆ Children's errors in reading reflect their understanding of written language.

◆ The teacher's role in instruction has changed from directing children's learning in literacy to supporting their development in literacy.

◆ Literacy is a social process.

◆ Children with book experiences before they enter school will generally do well in school as compared to children with little or no book experiences.

◆ Schema theory explains the importance of experiences and prior knowledge for comprehension.

With these thoughts in mind, let's now examine four broad areas of literacy learning more closely.

Understandings of Print Conventions

Print conventions refers to the arrangement of text on a page, print concepts, and text markings, such as punctuation or boldface type. These conventions critically influence the beginning reader and can be stumbling blocks if not taught explicitly. Clay (1991) focuses on this aspect of early literacy in much of her research, and devised the Concepts About Print assessment to help teachers understand and instruct in these important areas. Clay (1991) explains that the following understandings are necessary:

◉ the concepts of letter, word, picture, and sound

◉ the concepts that letters make up words and words make up sentences

◉ the meanings of punctuation marks

◉ how positional words, such as *first*, *last*, *beginning*, and *end*, apply to print, for example, how to identify the first letter in a word or the first word in a sentence

In addition to these general concepts about print, students must be aware of various arrangements of text and text markings. These print conventions can be words or letters in large or bold print, text that is formatted in a circular manner on the page, or text that is printed in various locations on the page. In order to support the beginning reader—who can easily be thrown off by such features—teachers can demonstrate how to read the conventions particular to a specific book and discuss what those conventions mean.

☀ Understandings of Word Recognition Development

Word recognition is the ability to read words, in isolation (sight words) and in context. For students to read fluently—a goal of literacy instruction—they must have a growing sight word vocabulary and be able to apply phonics skills and cueing strategies to unfamiliar words. In other words, they must have strong word recognition abilities.

Ehri (1994) discusses the developmental phases of this essential ability. First, students focus on the visual similarities and differences of words to read them. Next, they use sound/symbol relationships in addition to the visual cues to read words. At the most advanced phase, students use spelling patterns in their reading. Here are some examples of these phases:

Focus on visual differences:

Text - *Children like to play games during recess.* (Illustration shows children playing tag.) The student reads *games*, not *tag*, because of the differences in the words— namely, their lengths and initial consonants.

Focus on sound/symbol relationships:

Text - *I want to go to my home.* The student reads *home*, not *house*, because of the ending sounds in the words.

Focus on spelling patterns:

Text - *We found a rock on the ground.* The student reads *ground*, not *garden*, because of the spelling pattern of "ound."

Here is another way of looking at these phases: Children first use gross differences of words to distinguish them and gradually begin to focus on the details of words. Finally, they begin to recognize patterns in words or chunks of words. Usually the initial and final consonants are learned first, then the blends and digraphs, with the vowels coming in last. The pace at which children move through these phases into an efficient system of word recognition is partially dependent upon appropriate instruction.

It is important to remember that students need an understanding of language segmentation or breaks before the sound/symbol can be learned completely (Clay, 1991). The assessments in this book first assess students on word and syllable language segmentation and then later on sound segmenting. Word and syllable segmenting is important because it enables students to recognize individual words within sentences heard orally and helps them write words and sentences. Sound segmenting, or phonemic awareness, is crucial for the learning of the sound/symbol system.

To move through these phases to strong word recognition, students must have solid skills in letter recognition, print conventions, and phonemic awareness; these skills are predictors of success in learning to read and write (Adams, 1990). The assessments grouped under *Word Recognition* in this book help identify problems students may be having in these areas.

Here are some other important principles about word recognition to inform our teaching:

◆ For students to learn phonics, they must first develop an ear for the sounds of their language. They must also understand that words are made up of those sounds and that words can be broken apart into sounds (phonemic awareness) (Clay, 1991).

◆ When teaching phonics, it is more effective to teach whole words first, then to teach parts of words (Moustafa & Maldonado-Colon, 1999). Teach children the phonic patterns, not the generalizations (Johnston, 2001).

◆ Oral reading fluency, or reading automatically, is important to develop so that the memory can be freed to concentrate on higher levels of comprehension (Perfetti, 1985).

◆ Vocabulary development, especially of sight words, promotes oral reading fluency (Ehri, 1994).

◆ The ability to use meaning, structure, and visual (graphophonics or sound/symbol) cueing strategies is necessary for the development of oral reading fluency (Clay, 1993b; Fountas & Pinnell, 1996; Schulman & Payne, 2000).

Understandings of Comprehension Development

Comprehension is the goal of all reading. At the K–2 level, students often read literal level types of text. However, we can model key comprehension strategies during read aloud and shared reading and encourage students to use them in their independent and guided reading when appropriate. Here are some critical understandings about comprehension:

◉ Connecting reading to prior knowledge will promote learning (Anderson & Pearson, 1984).

◉ Self-monitoring for understanding will keep meaning as the focus of reading (Pearson, Roeher, Dole, & Duffy, 1992).

◉ Good readers ask themselves questions as they read (Pearson, Roeher, Dole, & Duffy, 1992).

◉ Good readers relate the learning from one text to another (Pearson, Roeher, Dole, & Duffy, 1992).

◎ Making inferences as one reads will improve thinking and reasoning (Pearson, Roeher, Dole, & Duffy, 1992).

◎ Understanding patterns of text and genre will assist in the understanding of the text being read (Taylor, 1992).

Keene and Zimmermann (1997) categorize these understandings into schema, questioning, determining importance in text, creating images, inferring, and synthesis. These key elements of comprehension instruction provide you with useful, concrete aspects to develop instructional activities. For example, if students are working on summarizing a story, you might have them draw pictures of the various events in the story, knowing that creating images will enhance their comprehension and ability to summarize. Moreover, these comprehension strategies can be modeled during read aloud and shared reading.

The assessments in this book evaluate beginning comprehension skills. These skills include understanding the events in a story (retelling), being able to complete the sentence structure of the story (cloze), identifying facts, and stating the problem and resolution of a story.

Understandings of Writing Development

Writing is a critical aspect of literacy instruction, but this book will primarily focus on the writing that is done during guided reading. While the emphasis during guided reading is, of course, reading, students do write—as they engage in word study and other activities, and, for older students, as they respond to text. Reading and writing are reciprocal, and integrating them makes for effective learning (Graves, 1994). In addition, guided reading groups provide the opportunity to focus on a small group of students and target their particular needs; it's an invaluable time for individualizing instruction, and it makes sense to incorporate and evaluate writing in this setting when appropriate. However, the writing instruction in guided reading does not replace the writing workshop time or the individual writing conferences that you may have with students. Writing workshop and shared and interactive writing involve the direct instruction necessary for students to develop composing abilities and practice writing skills.

In these grades we are helping children learn the mechanics of writing and how to compose a message to an audience. Some of the key understandings about writing are:

◆ writing develops in stages (Graves, 1983),

◆ writing and reading enhance each other (Cooper, 1993), and

◆ control over the mechanics of writing influences writing development; therefore, process and product are both important (Portalupi, 2000).

The last understanding is significant. Most young children do not have the ability to produce a mechanically correct piece. Therefore, there is a tendency to go one of two ways in instruction. Some teachers feel children need mechanical skills to write, so they focus on handwriting, spelling, punctuation, capitalization, and grammar. Others sense that fostering the process of writing is key to writing development, so they focus on teaching the writing process. However, as is true of the discussions in this book, a balance of both aspects is more effective in developing successful writers. Again, focus on the needs and strengths of your students to determine the priority and emphasis.

Expectations of Instruction in K–2

Taking these research findings and new understandings into consideration, it is evident that literacy instruction in grades K–2 should focus on four major areas: print conventions (how the print is arranged on the page, print concepts, and text markings such as punctuation or boldface type); word recognition development (skills involved in decoding text and word learning); comprehension development (understanding of text); and writing development (learning the mechanics of writing, as well as the ability to compose). In guided reading instruction, these four areas need to be in balance in order for a student to develop appropriately as a reader and writer. Often, teachers are unaware of small missteps in one or more of these areas that can cause a student to lag behind. Unaddressed, these missteps can impede progress in literacy development. That's why these assessments are so critical.

The expectations for the scope and sequence of instruction for each grade are included below. These expectations are based on the Skaneateles Elementary Language Arts Program, the Weaver Literacy Benchmark Program, and the New York State Standards in English Language Arts.

Kindergarten

At the kindergarten level, our expectations in each of these areas are for the students to begin their awareness of the reading and writing processes. Oral language fluency, or the ability to converse in English, is a basic prerequisite for learning to read and write in English. Children experiencing difficulty in speaking the language and understanding it will also experience difficulty in learning to read and write. Therefore, developing and refining students' oral language ability in kindergarten prepares them for reading and writing instruction. Children whose first language is not English often have difficulty in learning to read and write English, as do students with language difficulties. Children who have limited literacy experiences at home also need extra support. Some activities that enrich students' language experiences include read alouds, shared reading, literacy play centers, listening to taped stories, learning songs or poems with body movements, language experience stories, and language games.

In kindergarten, we expect children to master several key concepts about print conventions. These include the ability to locate the print on the page and to identify the cover of the book and its title. Students should understand which way to read, left to right with a return sweep; and recognize word boundaries, where a word begins and ends. Kindergartners also learn the names of letters and how to form letters. However, mastery of all 26 upper- and lowercase letter names and formations is not expected in this grade. Children are expected to identify and understand some punctuation, namely, the period and question mark. As they read text, they should be able to point to the words, demonstrating voice-print matching.

Kindergarten expectations for word recognition are limited to understanding that the story pictures help them read the words in the text (cueing strategy-meaning through pictures). Moreover, kindergartners need to understand that language is segmented into words and words into parts or syllables (phonemic awareness). In kindergarten, students are beginning to identify some basic words in print like *dog*, *cat*, *me*, *I*, *truck*, *run*, and their names.

For comprehension, we expect kindergartners to understand that print carries meaning and that the pictures help tell the story. They learn that all reading should make sense and that a book is true or fantasy. They can identify the topic or theme of a book. Some of the higher-level comprehension skills and strategies are modeled with the students in read aloud and shared reading, but in their simple texts children can make predictions of what the story is about and what comes next.

In writing, kindergartners are expected to write their first name with appropriate upper- and lowercase letters in addition to some other letters of the alphabet. They are also expected to write some words with invented spelling and some letters that represent words, such as *d* for *dad*. The letter-sound correspondence in their writing is minimal.

Aspects of Literacy Instruction for Kindergarten

Print Conventions

- Identify where the print is on the page
- Identify the cover of the book
- Identify the title of the book
- Understand which way to read (left to right)
- Identify the word boundaries of the print
- Demonstrate voice-print match
- Identify and understand purpose of period and question mark
- Identify the names of 45 out of 52 letters

Comprehension Development

- Understand that pictures help tell the story
- Understand that the book is true life or fantasy
- Identify the topic or theme of the book

Word Recognition Development

- Understand that pictures help tell the story
- Understand that the language is segmented into words and words into parts or syllables

Writing Development

- Write their first name with appropriate upper- and lowercase letters
- Write some letters of the alphabet
- Write some words with invented spelling and some letters that represent words, such as *d* for *dad*

 **Grade 1**

For first-grade students, our expectations expand to include not only the awareness of print but to actually reading print. First graders should understand what they read and use cueing strategies effectively.

For print conventions, first graders are expected to understand all the concepts from kindergarten. In addition, they begin to understand the meaning of boldface, italic, and all-caps type. They learn to identify and understand additional punctuation: the exclamation point, comma, and quotation marks. Students are able to follow the text as they or someone reads (voice-print match). First graders can identify all 26 upper- and lowercase letters.

For word recognition, first graders become familiar with meaning, structure, and visual or grapho-phonic (sound/symbol) cues. They are beginning to use all three cueing systems and their sight vocabulary grows rapidly. They still use picture clues, but they attend to the text as well. In phonics, they apply their knowledge of initial and final sounds along with short, long, and r-controlled vowels. They have the ability to sound segment words or to distinguish sounds in words; indeed, learning word patterns and using context are the primary ways children learn new words (Clay, 1993b). First graders are also self-correcting their errors as they read.

For comprehension, first graders rely extensively on their knowledge of the topic to keep the reading meaningful, making connections to their prior knowledge and experience. They are able to retell what they read. They can complete cloze sentences, which indicates their understanding of sentence structure and meaning. Cloze sentences are sentences taken from a reading but written with blanks replacing words of the story. Students fill in the blanks with meaningful words that reflect the story.

First graders are beginning to see text structures, such as sequence and description. They begin to identify story elements, such as problem and solution. It is expected that they understand the difference between fiction and nonfiction. Some genres are introduced to them at this grade level, including biographies, folk tales, fairy tales, informational articles, and poetry. First graders are becoming more focused on what the text is saying, not just on decoding it. Silent reading is part of the curriculum.

In writing, first graders can write simple sentences and use appropriate capitalization and punctuation. They can write all upper- and lowercase alphabet letters, and they begin to write simple stories of several sentences. They can respond to a writing prompt, although they do not always include complete details. They use their knowledge of phonics to spell words, but also have command of many spelling words. Conventional spelling is beginning to develop.

Aspects of Literacy Instruction for Grade 1

Print Conventions
- Understand how the text moves from line to line, or return sweep
- Understand the meaning of boldface, italic, and all-caps type
- Identify and understand punctuation: exclamation point, comma, quotation marks, in addition to periods and question marks
- Demonstrate voice-print match consistently
- Identify all 26 upper- and lowercase letters

Comprehension Development
- Rely on their knowledge of the topic they are reading to keep the reading meaningful (making connections)
- Able to retell and summarize reading
- Complete cloze sentences, which indicates understanding of story sentence structure
- Develop an understanding of text structures, such as sequence and description
- Begin to identify story elements, such as problem and resolution
- Understand the difference between fiction and nonfiction
- Understand some genres, including biographies, folk tales, fairy tales, informational articles, and poetry
- Utilize silent reading

Word Recognition Development
- Develop meaning, structure, and visual or grapho-phonic (sound/symbol) cueing strategies
- Begin to apply all three cueing systems and learn sight vocabulary
- Attend more to text than pictures
- Apply knowledge of initial and final sounds along with short, long, and r-controlled vowels
- Can segment words into sounds and distinguish sounds in words
- Self-correct their errors as they read
- Begin to read text with fluency, including expression

Writing Development
- Write simple sentences and use appropriate capitalization and punctuation
- Write all upper- and lowercase alphabet letters
- Write simple stories of several sentences
- Respond to a writing prompt, but do not always include complete details
- Use their knowledge of phonics to spell words, but also have command of several conventional spelling words

☀ Grade 2

Second graders are refining their reading and writing and becoming fluent. They can integrate and apply all cueing strategies, and they can write short chapter stories or reports.

In the area of print conventions, second graders are focused mostly on the text format and graphics. They are beginning to use and interpret graphs, graphic organizers, picture captions, indexes, the table of contents, and glossaries.

For word recognition, second graders become orally fluent and do much of their reading silently. They are able to integrate and apply meaning, structure, and visual (grapho-phonic) cues. They readily learn vocabulary from their reading. Second graders learn the meaning of affixes and how they can change the meanings of root or base words.

In terms of comprehension, second graders are becoming cognizant of literary elements, including title, author, genre, plot, climax, characters, and problem/ solution. They understand some of the elements of nonfiction text (format, content, graphics) and are beginning to understand fact versus opinion. They are developing an understanding of more text structures: time order, description, compare/contrast, cause/effect, and problem/solution. Second graders are also beginning to make connections with the text as well as beginning to make inferences from the text. For example, second graders can respond to "why" questions that require them to use the text they read and their own experiences. They begin to understand how each sentence in the text is related to the others to identify the author's purpose for writing. They can also identify the main idea of the text.

In writing, second graders are beginning to organize their writing and develop it more fully. They use more complex and varied sentence structures and include details or words (adjectives, adverbs) to write more vividly. Their spelling is predominantly conventional, although inventive spelling may be used for more sophisticated words. Second graders can proofread for simple sentence mechanics, such as capitals at the beginning of sentences and some proper nouns, and ending punctuation.

Aspects of Literacy Instruction for Grade 2

Print Conventions

- Understand different text formats and graphics
- Use and interpret graphs, graphic organizers, picture captions, indexes, the table of contents, and glossaries

Comprehension Development

- Develop an understanding of literary elements, including title, author, genre, plot, climax, characters, and problem/solution
- Understand some of the elements of nonfiction text (format, content, graphics)
- Develop an understanding of fact versus opinion
- Develop an understanding of text structures: time order, description, compare/contrast, cause/effect, and problem/solution
- Understand how to use the text and own experiences to make connections
- Begin to interpret or make connections with the text read and infer
- Identify the author's purpose for writing
- Identify main ideas in text
- Recall details of text

Word Recognition Development

- Achieve oral fluency
- Read much of their texts silently
- Integrate and apply meaning, structure, and visual (grapho-phonic) cueing strategies.
- Readily learn vocabulary from their reading
- Understand the meaning of affixes and how they can change the meaning of root or base words

Writing Development

- Attempt to organize writing and develop it more fully
- Use more complex and varied sentence structures
- Add details or words (adjectives, adverbs) to write more vividly
- Use predominantly conventional spelling, with invented spelling of more sophisticated words
- Proofread for simple sentence mechanics, such as capitals at the beginning of sentences and some proper nouns, and ending punctuation

 ## Balanced Guided Reading Instruction

As you prepare lesson plans for guided reading instruction, it is important to address all four aspects of literacy in each unit of study or book study. Too often primary teachers focus on oral reading fluency in guided reading and do not give adequate attention to comprehension and writing. All four of these areas are critical in literacy development at any age or grade level, especially in kindergarten through grade 2, and they need to be taught and assessed regularly.

Guided reading lessons using one book usually extend over three to five days in the primary grades depending on the length of the book and the various skills and strategies to be taught. To be most effective, these lessons need to focus specifically on the individual needs of the group. The teacher needs to intervene when a student begins to have trouble in an area and reteach the skill or strategy so that the student continues to progress. The remaining part of this book will provide you with the assessment tools and intervention strategies and activities you need to help improve your students' literacy development.

Chapter 6

Using Assessments to Keep Students Learning

The next three chapters present assessments for each grade level. They were designed to periodically evaluate the progress of students over the course of a school year. These performance assessments require students to demonstrate their ability to read and write. The criteria used to evaluate their work is based on feedback from the various school districts that have used these assessments and have documented the growth their students made. It is important to note that the criteria reflects the expectations of *average achieving students* at that grade level. Teachers will need to make their own decisions about students who have special needs.

These assessments target essential literacy competencies. Students not demonstrating these competencies will probably encounter difficulties at some time in learning to read or write. Therefore, it is critical that teachers assess all students to ensure success in literacy learning and to provide intervention instruction for those who need help developing the competencies.

What Are the Assessments?

For each grade level (K, 1, and 2), there are three assessments (A, B, and C) in addition to a diagnostic placement test for the grade. The diagnostic placement test uses aspects of the previous year's or week's assessments depending on the time of year. Kindergarten has a specific diagnostic placement test for the beginning of the school year because the assessments begin in kindergarten. At the beginning of each assessment chapter, there is a chart to help you find the appropriate diagnostic placement test.

The assessments at each grade level have six parts to them:

Diagnostic Placement Tests for Students Entering During School Year, Grade 1

Time of School Year	Diagnostic Placement Test to Use	Comments
Weeks 1–11	Kindergarten C Assessment	If most areas are too difficult for student, the Kindergarten B Assessment can be given
Weeks 13–23	Grade 1 A Assessment	Assessment items KCS.8 and KCS.9 on segmenting as well as KCW.12 and KCW.13 on letters should be given.
Weeks 25–35	Grade 1 B Assessment	Assessment items IAS.8 and IAS.9 on consonants should also be given
Week 37 to end of school year	Grade 1 C Assessment	Assessment items IBR.5 on vocabulary, IBS.6 on blends & digraphs, and IBS.7 on sound segmenting should also be given.

1. **Teacher Directions.** Gives you step-by-step procedures for administration of each assessment, time required, type of setting (group or individual), and the aspects being assessed.

2. **Assessment Book.** Found in the Appendix; blackline masters of the book in mini-book format for students to read.

3. **Rubrics.** These scoring rubrics help you identify and record a student's performance level for each task, from 1 (lowest) to 4 (highest). These rubrics help you judge whether the student performed adequately, exceptionally, or below grade level. The RTI Benchmark Chart is found after the rubrics for each assessment. This chart identifies the level of intensity of instruction. You can then use this information to plan further instruction.

4. **Individual Student Profile.** Records student performance on the assessments throughout the year.

5. **Student Response Sheets.** These sheets are necessary in the administration of the assessment. The students write or point on these sheets. Some of the sheets are used to record the task done, such as a running record of the assessment book.

6. **Class Record Sheet.** (See Appendix, p. 193.) You can record the class' scores on this sheet and see their instructional needs at a glance.

When given regularly, these assessments can inform instruction by pinpointing students' difficulties and strengths. You can differentiate instruction more accurately to fit the needs of your students. In addition, you can record a class' performance on the class record sheet found in the Appendix to get an overview of the class' needs and abilities.

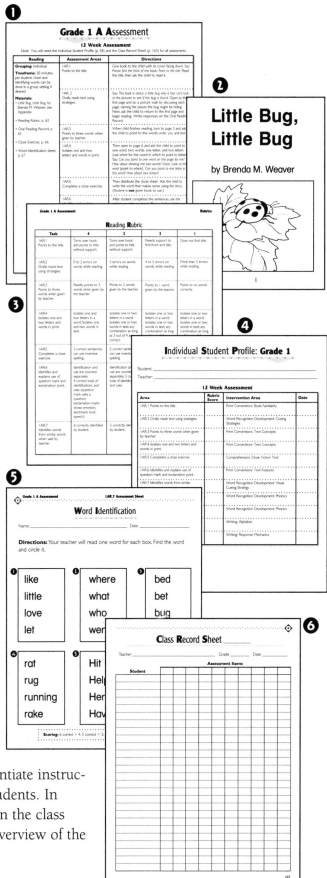

❋ What Do the Assessments Evaluate?

The assessments evaluate various skills, strategies, and concepts children must have to progress as readers and writers. These are described fully in Chapter 3. The four main categories are Print Conventions; Word Recognition, including vocabulary, reading cueing strategies, and phonics; Comprehension; and Writing. The following chart summarizes what is assessed when.

Grade/Assessment	Print Conventions	Word Recognition	Comprehension	Writing
KA or 12th Week (KA)	Identifies front and back of book; points to print on page; demonstrates voice-print match; knows directionality (left to right).		Tells topic of book.	Writes name; identifies letters in name.
KB or 24th Week (KB)	Identifies title; knows directionality; demonstrates voice-print match; identifies period; counts words and letters in text.	Uses picture cues; segments words and letters.	Tells details of book.	Draws picture that relates to topic; attempts to label or writes words for story; recognizes letters; writes letters.
KC or 36th Week (KC)	Identifies title; knows directionality; demonstrates voice-print match; identifies question mark; counts words and letters in text.	Uses picture cues; segments words and letters.	Tells details of book.	Draws picture that relates to topic; attempts to label or writes words for story; recognizes letters; writes letters.
1A or 12th Week (1A)	Identifies title; points to given words; isolates letters and words; identifies period, question mark, exclamation point.	Uses meaning and structure cues while reading; identifies similar words; identifies initial and final consonants.	Completes cloze exercise to demonstrate comprehension.	Writes letters of alphabet; writes a response with some attempt at sentences.
1B or 24th Week (1B)	Identifies comma, quotation marks.	Uses meaning, structure, and visual (phonics) cues while reading; reads familiar sight vocabulary words; segments sounds in words (phonemic awareness); identifies blends and digraphs.	Completes cloze exercise to demonstrate comprehension; retells story.	Writes a simple story.
1C or 36th Week (1C)		Uses meaning, structure, and visual (phonics) cues while reading; reads words by applying long, short, and r-controlled vowel patterns (phonics); identifies contractions; uses word endings.	Completes cloze exercise to demonstrate comprehension; responds to book in writing.	Writes a personal response with a minimum of five sentences.

Grade/Assessment	Print Conventions	Word Recognition	Comprehension	Writing
2A or 12th Week (2A)		Uses meaning, structure, and visual (phonics) cues while reading; reads nonsense words by applying double vowel patterns (phonics).	Retells the story in writing.	Writes a story with a beginning, middle, and end.
2B or 24th Week (2B)		Recognizes and reads words with prefixes and suffixes.	Writes a brief retelling of story with main events; completes a cloze exercise (processing of text for meaning); identifies characters and their attributes.	Writes a literary response with supporting details from the book.
2C or 36th Week (2C)			Identifies facts; identifies problem/solution.	Writes a literary response with supporting details from the book.

How Are the Assessments Administered?

These assessments can easily fit into the routine of a balanced literacy classroom. I recommend administering them during guided reading. Assessing all students individually takes about a week of guided reading time, although some of the assessments can be done in a group setting. The Teacher Directions provided for each assessment indicate the ideal grouping and approximate time frame for each task.

When you administer the assessments, it is important to perform the tasks as directed without providing any additional support, so that the results are valid from child to child. If a child becomes too frustrated with a task, simply stop the testing and indicate that the task was too difficult for the child. These assessments are tools to help teachers evaluate students' progress and then make appropriate instructional choices. Compromising the testing environment detracts from the instructional decision-making and frustrates students.

Some of the assessment tasks require specific knowledge of certain assessment techniques. I recommend taking a running record for each assessment starting with the 24 week Kindergarten Assessment. This powerful assessment tool was developed by Marie Clay and is described fully in *An Observation Survey of Early Literacy Achievement* (1993a). You can find the forms and directions there for taking running records. Alternatively, you can assess students' reading with the Oral Reading Record form I have provided here. Word lists can assess sight vocabulary knowledge, or the ability to say words without decoding them, and decoding ability. For sight vocabulary assessment, encourage students to not sound out the words but to say them quickly. For decoding word assessments, encourage students to look carefully at the words and sound them out. When preparing book introductions, the approach you take will depend on the purpose of the assessment. For kindergarten, the purpose of the introduction is to assist with picture cues and vocabulary, while in grade 2 the purpose is more of relating the text content to prior knowledge. The specific directions and scoring criteria are included in the teacher assessment sheets, recording sheets, and scoring rubrics.

☑ Specific Steps for Administering the Assessments

Begin by administering the diagnostic test for the grade early in the year. This will establish a baseline for each student and guide your teaching in those first few weeks. Also plan to administer the rest of the formal assessments: I recommend administering the 12 week Assessment during the 13th week of school, the 24 week Assessment during the 25th week, and the 36 week Assessment during the 37th week. Here are the specific steps for giving the assessments:

1. Gather the appropriate materials for your students; these are listed on each assessment.

2. Administer any group assessments to the whole class or to small groups.

3. Administer the individual tests to the students.

4. Use the scoring rubrics to score the assessments. Put the scores on the Individual Student Profile and the Class Record Sheet (found in the Appendix). Mark the strengths and weaknesses of the students according to the assessments. The strengths are the items on which the student scored a 3 or 4 on the rubric, while the weaknesses are the items on which the student scored a 1 or a 2. For the 1 and 2 scores, highlight the appropriate intervention area for instruction. Check the RTI Benchmark Charts to determine if the instruction intensity or methods need adjustments.

5. Plan the intervention instruction for the students based on the 1 and 2 score areas. Find the appropriate activities, techniques, or approaches in the intervention chapters. When the students seem to have acquired the skills or strategies, re-administer the specific items on the assessment to determine if they met the criteria. If they have, they are ready for all of the challenges of the next level. Note: Students who get a 1 or 2 on the Oral Reading Record need to continue their instruction at that book level until they get a 3 or 4 on the evaluation. (See the chart on book levels for instruction in Chapter 12.) Teachers may want to use another assessment book at the same assessment book level from a publisher for the retest.

6. If there are no intervention areas (all scores were 3 or 4), plan for the next harder level of instruction and book level. (See the chart on book levels for instruction in Chapter 12.)

✸ Special Needs Students

All heterogeneous classrooms will have students who are not able to read the text at the designated time or who can read well beyond the designated assessment. Make alterations in the assessment schedule to accommodate these students.

For students who get 4s on all of the items in the 12 Week Assessment, administer the 24 Week Assessment to see if any instructional areas need intervention. If the grade-level assessments are all 4s on the scoring, then you can administer the next grade-level assessments. If you are in grade 2 and your student takes all three assessments and scores all 4s, then you know this student has acquired all the necessary competencies to be a successful reader and writer in grade 2. You'll need to provide more challenging instruction in language arts at a higher reading level.

For students who are not able to read the text or perform any tasks with any success, you will want to use the assessments at the previous grade level. If you have students in kindergarten who cannot perform the tasks at week 12, then indicate that at this time they were unable to demonstrate any competencies, and do not test them. Later in the kindergarten year, try the Kindergarten A Assessment. The limited progress of these students will need to be noted on their Individual Student Profile for next year's teacher. The next year's teacher can then begin the assessments where the kindergarten teacher stopped. The same procedure can be followed in grades 1 and 2. The documentation helps teachers provide appropriate instruction as students move up the grades.

✸ Looking Ahead

This chapter has given you an overview of how these assessments can be used to assess the strengths and weaknesses of students in grades K–2. The specific assessments are presented in the next three chapters. These assessment chapters include the directions, scoring rubrics, and student response sheets necessary for each assessment.

Chapter 7

Kindergarten Assessments

At the beginning of the school year, teachers assess the needs of their students to establish a baseline and plan appropriate instruction. Kindergarten is special because it is often students' first formal school experience, although more and more children are attending preschool. With students arriving with diverse experiences and abilities, it is essential to assess them as soon as possible to get an overview of the class. The Kindergarten Diagnostic Placement Test allows you to immediately evaluate children's book-handling skills and determine if they can read or write anything. I recommend administering it within the first few weeks of school. Use the evaluation checklist on page 58 to identify the needs of individual students and then record the class' scores on the Class Record Sheet (p.193) to see an overview of the class' current abilities.

The subsequent kindergarten assessments focus primarily on book handling skills, knowledge of the alphabet, and awareness of language segmenting, all understandings kindergartners develop during the year; see Chapter 5 for details. Each assessment uses a book found in the Appendix in mini-book format. Each book is progressively more challenging, allowing you to assess an increasing range of competencies over the course of the year. The following chart compares the reading levels of the kindergarten assessment books.

Approximate Reading Levels for Kindergarten Assessment Books

Assessment	Weaver Literacy Levels	Guided Reading Levels*	Schulman and Payne Levels	Reading Recovery Levels	Traditional Basal Levels
K Diagnostic Placement	Emergent A (EmA)	A	Emergent	I	Readiness
12th Week or KAR	Emergent A (EmA)	A	Emergent	I	Readiness
24th Week or KBR	Emergent B (EmB)	B	Emergent	2	Readiness
36th Week or KCR	Emergent B (EmB)	B–C	Emergent	2–3	Readiness

Note: These are approximate levels due to the variety of leveling systems and the inability to have direct relationships between the leveling systems.

* Guided Reading Levels as described by Fountas and Pinnell in *Guided Reading* (1996).

The average kindergartner progressing at an average rate will score at the 3 level on each task for each assessment. Students scoring at the 4 level will need to be challenged in instruction, while students scoring in the 1 to 2 range need intervention and retesting on those items in order to ensure adequate development. The intervention area is listed on the Individual Student Profile, and you'll find appropriate techniques and activities to address specific needs in the designated intervention chapter.

The Scoring Sheets

You will find two types of scoring sheets to help you make the most of the data you collect with the assessments. There is a kindergarten Individual Student Profile, on which you record specific information about individual students. This format allows you to see their growth over the course of a year. In addition, you will find a Class Record Sheet in the Appendix (p. 193). I recommend preparing one of these for your class; it will summarize the class' performance, giving you an at-a-glance view of their overall weaknesses and strengths. In addition, the RTI Benchmark Chart will recommend the adjustments in instruction or support necessary at this time.

In kindergarten, most assessments are administered individually. The total time needed per child is approximately 30 minutes. A few of the tasks can be done in a small group; the recommended grouping is listed with each task. I suggest allotting a week's worth of reading time to complete the assessments.

A note about the assessments: Each item to be assessed is given a label for ease of reference. The first character indicates the grade level; for the kindergarten assessments, all assessment items begin with K. The second character indicates which assessment it belongs to (A, B, or C, meaning the 12 Week, 24 Week, and 36 Week Assessment, respectively) and the third character references the assessment area. For instance, KAR indicates an item from the Kindergarten A Assessment that evaluates a reading skill. In addition, each item within an assessment area is then numbered to differentiate the tasks. In the Kindergarten A Assessment, there are five items that assess reading skills, and they are numbered KAR.1–KAR.5. In each assessment, the tasks are numbered this way, and the rubrics, scoring guides, and record sheets use the same labeling system.

Tip

Highlight scores of 1 and 2 on the Class Record Sheet for a quick view of instructional areas that need immediate attention.

Diagnostic Placement Tests for Students Entering During School Year

Time of School Year	Diagnostic Placement Test to Use	Comments
Weeks 1–11	Kindergarten Diagnostic Placement Test	Use as a baseline for entering students.
Weeks 13–23	Kindergarten A Assessment	If most areas are too difficult for student, the Kindergarten Diagnostic Placement Test can be given.
Weeks 25–35	Kindergarten B Assessment	If most areas are too difficult for student, the Kindergarten A Assessment can be given.
Week 37 to end of school year	Kindergarten C Assessment	If most areas are too difficult for student, the Kindergarten B or A Assessments can be given.

Individual Student Profile: Kindergarten

Student: _____

Teacher: _____

Diagnostic Assessment

Area	Yes or No	Intervention Area/Comments	Date
K 1 Holds the book appropriately.		Print Conventions	
K 2 Points to print on page.		Print Conventions	
K 3 Reads any words.		Word Recognition	
K 4 Speaking language is appropriate for kindergarten (speaks with appropriate grammar and in sentences).		Oral Language	
K 5 Writes name.		Writing	
K 6 Identifies letters in name in print.		Writing	
K 7 Draws/writes about topic.		Writing	

Individual Student Profile: Kindergarten

Student: _____

Teacher: _____

12 Week Assessment

Task	Rubric Score	Intervention Area/Comments	Date
KAR.1 Finds front of book; finds back of book.		Print Conventions: Book Familiarity	
KAR.2 Understands print is on page.		Print Conventions: Book Familiarity	
KAR.3 Follows story read.		Print Conventions: Text Concepts	
KAR.4 Knows reading goes from left to right.		Print Conventions: Book Familiarity	
KAR.5 Understands topic of book.		Comprehension: Retelling/Summarizing; Fiction	
KAW.6 Writes name.		Writing: Alphabet	
KAW.7 Spells name.		Writing: Alphabet	

Individual Student Profile: Kindergarten

Student: _____

Teacher: _____

24 Week Assessment

Task	Rubric Score	Intervention Area	Date
KBR.1 Points to title.		Print Conventions: Book Familiarity	
KBR.2 Understands directionality/ voice-print match.		Print Conventions: Book Familiarity; Text Concepts	
KBR.3 Reads fluently.		Word Recognition: Cueing Strategies	
KBR.4 Identifies period with purpose.		Print Conventions: Text Features	
KBR.5 Counts words in sentence.		Print Conventions: Text Concepts	
KBR.6 Counts letters in word.		Print Conventions: Text Concepts	
KBR.7 Tells details of book.		Comprehension: Detail; Nonfiction Text	
KBR.8 Segments words in sentences.		Word Recognition: Segmentation	
KBR.9 Segments syllables in words.		Word Recognition: Segmentation	
KBW.10 Identifies letters in name and words.		Writing: Alphabet	
KBW.11 Draws picture to convey meaning.		Writing: Story; Mechanics	
KBW.12 Writes names on paper and letters to make words about picture.		Writing: Story; Mechanics	
KBW.13 Identifies letters.		Writing: Alphabet	
KBW.14 Writes letters.		Writing: Alphabet	

Individual Student Profile: Kindergarten

Student: _____

Teacher: _____

36 Week Assessment

Task	Rubric Score	Intervention Area	Date
KCR.1 Points to title.		Print Conventions: Book Familiarity	
KCR.2 Understands directionality/ voice-print match.		Print Conventions: Book Familiarity; Text Concepts	
RCR.3 Reads fluently.		Word Recognition: Cueing Strategies	
KCR.4 Identifies question mark with purpose.		Print Conventions: Text Features	
KCR.5 Counts words in sentence.		Print Conventions: Text Concepts	
KCR.6 Counts letters in word.		Print Conventions: Text Concepts	
KBR.7 Tells details of book.		Comprehension: Detail; Nonfiction Text	
KCR.8 Segments words in sentences.		Word Recognition: Segmentation	
KCR.9 Segments syllables in words.		Word Recognition: Segmentation	
KCW.10 Draws picture to convey meaning.		Writing: Story; Mechanics	
KCW.11 Writes letters to make words about picture.		Writing: Story; Mechanics	
KCW.12 Identifies letters.		Writing: Alphabet	
KCW.13 Writes letters.		Writing: Alphabet	

RTI Benchmark Charts: Kindergarten

12 Week

- Adequate Progress = Continue with present program
- Adjust Instruction = More small-group instruction with different materials/methods are necessary
- Outside Support = Student requires additional evaluation by support personnel and possible testing

Adequate Progress	Adjust Instruction	Outside Support
No more than two items scored at 2 or below	KBR.2 or KBR.3 scored at 2 or below AND one or two of other items scored at 2 or below	KBR.2 and KBR.3 scored at 2 or below AND three or more other items scored at 2 or below

24 Week

- Adequate Progress = Continue with present program
- Adjust Instruction = More small-group instruction with different materials/methods are necessary
- Outside Support = Student requires additional evaluation by support personnel and possible testing

Adequate Progress	Adjust Instruction	Outside Support
No more than two items scored at 2 or below	KBR.2 or KBR.3 scored at 2 or below AND one or two of other items scored at 2 or below	KBR.2 and KBR.3 scored at 2 or below AND three or more other items scored at 2 or below

36 Week

- Adequate Progress = Continue with present program
- Adjust Instruction = More small-group instruction with different materials/methods are necessary
- Outside Support = Student requires additional evaluation by support personnel and possible testing

Adequate Progress	Adjust Instruction	Outside Support
No more than two items scored at 2 or below	Three of the following scored at 2 or below: KCR.2, KCR.3, KCR.8, KCR.9, KCW.11, KCW.12 AND one or two of the other items scored at 2 or below	All of the following scored at 2 or below: KCR.2, KCR.3, KCR.8, KCR.9, KCW.11, KCW.12 AND one or two of the other items scored at 2 or below

Kindergarten Diagnostic Placement Test

Note: You will need the Individual Student Profile (p. 58) and Class Record Sheet (p. 193) for all assessments.

Reading	Assessment Areas	Directions
Grouping: Individual **Timeframe:** 15 minutes **Materials:** • *I Like Fruit* by Brenda M. Weaver; see Appendix • Individual Student Profile, p. 58	K 1 Holds the book appropriately.	Give book to the child turned over with cover face down. Ask: *If you were going to read this book, how would you hold it? Show me.*
	K 2 Points to print on page.	Point to words in the title and read the title aloud. Explain that the book is about different kinds of fruit. Then open to pages 2 and 3. Read these pages aloud and have the child point to the words. Say: *Point to the words while I read these pages to you.*
	K 3 Reads any words.	Read page 4. Then turn to page 5, point to it and ask: *Can you read any of the words on this page?* Turn to page 6 and say: *Try to read this page for me.* Child reads page 6 and continues to read if capable. Otherwise, you read the rest of the book as the child points to the words.
	K 4 Speaking language is appropriate for kindergarten (speaks with appropriate grammar and in sentences).	Finish reading the book aloud. Then ask: *Is there a fruit that you like to eat? What is it? Tell me why you like it.*
Reading	**Assessment Areas**	**Directions**
Grouping: Individual or small group **Timeframe:** 15–20 minutes **Materials:** • Stationery A, p. 194 • Individual Student Profile, p. 58	K 5 Writes name. K 6 Identifies letters in name in print.	Point to the paper and say: *Can you write your name here?* When the child is done, ask: *Can you tell me the letters in your name?*
	K 7 Draws/Writes about topic.	Ask the child to draw a picture and/or write about something he or she likes to eat.

Kindergarten A Assessment

12 Week Assessment

Note: You will need the Individual Student Profile (p. 59) and Class Record Sheet (p. 193) for all assessments.

Reading	Assessment Areas	Directions
Grouping: Individual **Timeframe:** 15 minutes per student **Materials:** • *I Like to Eat Food*, by Brenda M. Weaver (see Appendix) • Reading Rubric, p. 65	KAR. 1 Finds front of book; finds back of book.	Give book to the child turned over with cover face down. Say: *Find the front of the book. Find the back of the book.*
	KAR. 2 Understands print is on page.	Point to words in the title and read the title aloud. Explain that the book is about different kinds of food. Open the book to pages 4 and 5. Ask: *Point to the print.*
	KAR. 3 Follows a story read aloud using print.	Go back to the beginning of the book and ask the child to point to the words as you read. Read pages 2 and 3, supporting the child in pointing. Then turn to pages 4 and 5 and read without supporting the child in pointing to the words. Finish reading the book, having the child point to words without support.
	KAR. 4 Knows reading goes from left to right.	Go back to pages 6 and 7 and ask: *Where do we start to read?*
	KAR. 5 Understands general topic of book.	After reading the story ask: *What is this story about?*
Writing	**Assessment Areas**	**Directions**
Grouping: Individual **Timeframe:** 5 minutes per student **Materials:** • Stationery A, p. 194	KAW. 6 Writes name.	Ask the child to write his or her name on the paper.
	KAW. 7 Identifies letters in name in print.	Ask the child to point to letters in his or her name and say them aloud.

Reading Rubric

Task	4	3	2	1
KAR.1 Finds front of book; finds back of book.	Turns over book and points to front and back without support.	Needs support to turn over book and point to front and back.	Points to back for front or front for back.	Does not understand.
KAR.2 Understands print is on page.	Points to print on page where you start to read.	Points to any print on page.	Does not seem to know where print is, but then points to some.	Does not point to print.
KAR.3 Follows story read.	Readily points to the words without hesitation and is accurate.	Points to the print but hesitates or misses 1 or 2 words.	Points to print but does not follow word by word.	Cannot follow print.
KAR.4 Tracks left to right.	Readily points to left-hand page and beginning of sentence.	Hesitates and points to left-hand page and/or print but not at beginning of line.	Points to print on right-hand page.	Cannot decide or points to picture.
KAR.5 Understands topic of book.	Readily says that the book is about all kinds of food and names some.	Explains that it is about cookies, etc. (names individual foods); more than 2 foods recalled.	Reluctantly responds and names 1 or 2 foods.	No response.

Writing Rubric

Task	4	3	2	1
KAR.6 Writes name; finds back of book.	Writes name with correct letters, including appropriate upper- and lowercase letters.	Writes name with correct letters but name is mixed with upper- and lowercase letters.	Writes name but has 1 or 2 errors in letters and letters can be mixed with upper- and lowercase letters.	Writes name with more than 2 errors in letters **or** unable to do task.
KAR.7 Spells name.	Identifies all letters in name by spelling.	Identifies more than 50% but not 100% of letters in name by spelling.	Identifies 50% of letters in name by spelling.	Identifies less than 50% of letters in name by spelling **or** unable to do task.

Kindergarten B Assessment

24 Week Assessment

Note: You will need the Individual Student Profile (p. 60) and Class Record Sheet (p. 193) for all assessments.

Reading	Assessment Areas	Directions
Grouping: Individual **Timeframe:** 15 minutes per student **Materials:** • *At the Zoo* by Brenda M. Weaver; see Appendix • Reading Rubric, p. 68 • Oral Reading Record, p. 70	KBR.1 Points to title.	Give book to the child turned over. Ask: *Please find the front of the book. Can you point to the title?* Then read the title and have the child read it.
	KBR. 2 Understands directionality and points to words as reading.	Say: *This book is about animals at the zoo. Let's look at the pictures to see the animals at the zoo.* Turn to the first page and do a picture walk by discussing the animals shown in the text, naming each one. Then ask the child to return to the first page and point to the text while you read the first sentence.
	KBR. 3 Remembers sentence stem and uses pictures as a cueing strategy.	Ask the child to read the rest of the book while you take an oral reading record. Note if the child uses picture cues effectively.
	KBR. 4 Identifies period and gives purpose.	Turn to page 3 and ask the child to point to a period. Then ask: *What does a period tell you to do in reading?*
	KBR. 5 Counts words in sentence.	Ask the child to count the number of words in the sentence on page 3.
	KBR. 6 Counts letters in a word.	On page 4, point to the word *monkeys* and ask the child to count the letters.
	KBR. 7 Tells details of the book.	Finally, close the book and ask the child to name some animals at the zoo. Say something like: *That was a fun book! What was your favorite animal? What were some other animals at the zoo?*
Segmenting	**Assessment Areas**	**Directions**
Grouping: Small group or individual **Timeframe:** 10 minutes **Materials:** • Segmentation: Sentences to Words, p. 71 • Segmentation: Words to Syllables, p. 72 • Segmenting/Writing/Letters Rubric, p. 69	KBS. 8 Segments words in sentences.	See Segmentation: Sentences to Words (p. 71) for directions.
	KBS. 9 Segments syllables in words.	See Segmentation: Words to Syllables (p. 72) for directions.

24 Week Assessment (cont.)

Note: You will need the Individual Student Profile (p. 60) and Class Record Sheet (p.193) for all assessments.

Writing	Assessment Areas	Directions
Grouping: Individual **Timeframe:** 10 minutes per student **Materials:** • Stationery A, p. 194 or blank lined paper • Segmenting/Writing/ Letters, Rubric, p. 69	KBW.10 Identifies letters in name and words.	Ask the child to write his or her name on the line on the paper. Open *At the Zoo* to pages 6 and 7 and ask the child to spell the words *tigers* and *lions* while looking at the words.
Grouping: Small group **Timeframe:** 10–15 minutes **Materials:** • Stationery B, p. 195	KBW. 11 Draws picture to convey meaning. KBW. 12 Writes name on paper and letters to make words about picture.	Ask children to write their names on paper on the line. You write the date. Then say: *Draw a picture of something you like to do outside. Then on the lines below, write about your picture.*
Grouping: Individual **Timeframe:** 10 minutes **Materials:** • Letter Recognition Presentation Sheet, p. 198 • Letter Recognition Scoring Sheet, p. 197	KBW. 13 Identifies letters.	Show student Letter Recognition Presentation Sheet on page 198. Say: *Tell me the letters on this sheet.*
Grouping: Small group **Timeframe:** 15 minutes **Materials:** • Writing the Alphabet, p. 200 • Writing the Alphabet Teacher Directions, p. 199	KBW. 14 Writes letters.	Give Writing the Alphabet sheet to children and ask them to write letters. Say: *I will say a letter. Write the upper- and lowercase letter (big and small letter) in one box. Let's try the first one.* [Point to first box.] *Write the upper- and lowercase c in this box.* Continue in the same manner for the rest of the letters.

Reading Rubric

Task	4	3	2	1
KBR.1 Finds title.	Turns over book and points to title without support.	Turns over book and needs support to point to title.	Needs support to find front and title.	Does not find title.
KBR.2 Understands directionality/voice-print match.	Points to print on page when reading and goes from one page to another.	Needs some support to read from page to page and does not always show voice-print match.	Gets confused from page to page and does not demonstrate voice-print match.	Does not point to print.
KBR.3 Reads fluently.	0 to 1 error on words while reading.	2 errors on words while reading.	3 or 4 errors on words while reading.	More than 4 errors while reading.
KBR.4 Identifies period with purpose.	Readily points to period and says it tells you to stop when reading.	Able to identify period but cannot give purpose or says the opposite.	Not able to find period.	Not able to find period.
KBR.5 Counts words in sentence.	Counts accurately.	Counts accurately.	Counts inaccurately but is off by 1 word only, i. e., says 4 words or 2 words.	No response or totally incorrect.
KBR.6 Counts letters in word.	Counts accurately.	Counts accurately.	Counts inaccurately but is off by 1 letter only.	No response or totally incorrect.
KBR.7 Tells details of book.	Relates 4 or more animals at the zoo.	Relates 3 animals at the zoo.	Relates 1 or 2 animals at the zoo.	No response.

Segmenting/Writing/Letters Rubric

Task	4	3	2	1
KBS.8 Segments words in sentences.	All correct.	4 correct out of 5 sentences.	3 correct out of 5 sentences.	Fewer than 3 correct.
KBS.9 Segments syllables in words.	All correct.	4 correct out of 5 words.	3 correct out of 5 words.	Fewer than 3 correct.
KBW.10 Identifies letters in name and words.	Spells all words and name correctly.	Spells name correctly and misses only 1 letter in word spelling.	Spells name incorrectly and makes only 2 or 3 errors on word spelling.	More than 4 errors on words and spells name incorrectly.
KBW.11 Draws picture to convey meaning.	Picture has a great deal of detail which is relevant to topic.	Picture is relevant to topic and has some detail.	Picture is sketchy and has little detail.	No picture, irrelevant picture, or very sparse picture that is difficult to understand.
KBW.12 Writes name on paper and letters to make words about picture.	Writes name on paper correctly with upper- and lower-case letters. Writes a simple "sentence" or more using clusters of letters to represent words.	Writes name on paper correctly with upper- and lower-case letters. Writes some clusters of letters to represent words and thoughts. Clusters are 2 or more letters.	Name is inaccurate. Writes only 1 or 2 clusters of letters, maybe only 1 letter to represent words.	Name is inaccurate. No writing or a letter or two for writing.
KBW.13 Identifies letters.	Identifies over 40 letters.	Identifies 40 out of 52 letters.	Identifies 30–39 out of 52 letters.	Identifies fewer than 30 letters.
KBW.14 Writes letters.	Writes more than 35 letters correctly (reversing letters is acceptable—see test sheet for scoring).	Writes 35 out of 52 letters correctly (reversing letters is acceptable—see test sheet for scoring).	Writes 10–14 out of 52 letters correctly (reversing letters is acceptable—see test sheet for scoring).	Writes fewer than 10 letters correctly.

Oral Reading Record

Name _____ Date _____

Directions: Ask the child to read the mini-book aloud; record any mistakes here. Put a check (✓) over words read correctly and circle words omitted. If a word is mispronounced or a substitution is made, write the incorrect word over the correct word. If you had to say the word for the child, write T above the word. If an error is repeated over and over again (such as reading *look* for *like* in every sentence), count it as *one error*. If the child says *look* for *like* on one page, reads *like* correctly on the next, and then reads *look* for *like* on another page, count each error. Record your observations about the child's reading behaviors in the comments box.

24 Week Book — *At the Zoo* by Brenda M. Weaver

Text	Comments
There are elephants.	
There are zebras.	
There are monkeys.	
There are snakes.	
There are tigers.	
There are lions.	
There are parrots.	
All are at the zoo.	

Scoring Guide
Orally read with 0–1 errors = 4; 2 errors = 3; 3–4 errors = 2; more than 4 errors = 1.

Segmentation: Sentences to Words

Name _____ Date _____

Directions: Gather a set of blocks (15 or so) or small items and place them on the desk or table where the child is seated. Tell the child that you will read a sentence aloud. Then ask the child to repeat the sentence and move one block out for each word he or she says. It is important for the child to say aloud the words as he or she segments the sentences so you can appropriately score the response; see the scoring guide below. It is acceptable for the child to move one block per word or per syllable. However, the child must at least correctly segment by words. You may repeat the sentence if there was some sort of interference, such as noise or talking, that distracted the child. You can use the practice items to model the task. Record scores on the Individual Student Profile.

Scoring Guide for Sentence Segmentation

Give one point for each correctly segmented sentence with no errors; put a check next to each correct sentence. Put a 0 for a sentence with any errors. The possible number of blocks is in parentheses after the sentence. If a child makes an error on one sentence, present the corresponding retest sentence. If the child segments the retest sentence correctly, award a point and disregard the error on the initial sentence.

Count each of the following as one error:

- Child cannot remember the sentence.

- Child uses one block for two words. For example, if the child says *like* and moves two blocks, it is one error.

- Child omits a word or words.

The following are not counted as errors:

- Child substitutes a word in the sentence but moves a block for it. For example, if you say *Tim ran* and the child repeats, *Tim swam* and moves two blocks, there are no errors.

- Child moves blocks by syllable. For example, in *Today is Sunday*, if a child moves two blocks for /sun/ and /day/, do not count it as an error. But if a child moves two blocks for *is*, do count it as an error.

Practice Sentences

_____ **Tim ran.**

_____ **Today is Sunday.**

Test Sentences

1. _____ Come here. (2)

2. _____ Tom ran home. (3)

3. _____ I want to run. (4)

4. _____ Sue wants to go fishing. (5–6)

5. _____ Mary is going to the store. (6–8)

Retest Sentences

1. _____ He fell. (2)

2. _____ Jake likes food. (3)

3. _____ I like to eat. (4)

4. _____ Pam went to see grandma. (5–6)

5. _____ Sally is eating her lunch outside. (6–9)

Scoring: 5 correct out of 5 = 4; 4 correct out of 5 = 3; 3 correct out of 5 = 2; fewer than 3 correct = 1

Segmentation: Words to Syllables

Name _____ Date _____

Directions: Gather a set of blocks (5 or so) or small items for the child to use for segmenting words and place them on the desk or table where the child is seated. Tell the child that you will read a word aloud. Ask the child to repeat the word and move one block out for each syllable in the word. It is important for the child to say aloud the words as they are segmented so you can appropriately score the responses. You may repeat the word if there was some sort of interference, such as noise or talking, that distracted the child. You can use the practice items to model the task. Record scores on the Individual Student Profile.

Scoring Guide for Word Segmentation Task

Give one point for each correctly segmented word. If a child cannot segment a word into syllables, mark the item with a 0. The possible number of blocks is given in parentheses after each word.

Practice Words

1. _____ happy (2)
2. _____ doghouse (2)
3. _____ tomorrow (3)

Task Words

1. _____ summer (2)
2. _____ elephant (3)
3. _____ classmate (2)
4. _____ gingerbread (3)
5. _____ father (2)

Scoring: 5 correct out of 5 = 4; 4 correct out of 5 = 3; 3 correct out of 5 = 2; less than 3 correct = 1

Kindergarten C Assessment

36 Week Assessment

Note: Individual Student Profile (p. 61) and the Class Record Sheet (p. 193) needed for all assessments.

Reading	Assessment	Directions
Grouping: Individual **Timeframe:** 20 minutes per student **Materials:** • *Fish* by Brenda M. Weaver; see Appendix • Reading Rubric, p. 75 • Oral Reading Record, p. 77	KCR.1 Points to title.	Give book to the child turned over. Ask: *Please find the front of the book. Can you point to the title?* Then read the title and have the child read it.
	KCR. 2 Understands directionality and points to words as reading.	Say: *This book is about different kinds of fish. Let's look at the pictures to see the different kinds of fish.* Open to the first page and do a picture walk by discussing each fish and its characteristics described in the text. On the last page, discuss with the child what the fish are doing in the picture (swimming). Then ask the child to return to the first page.
	KCR. 3 Remembers sentence stem and uses pictures as a cueing strategy.	Say: *I will read the first sentence. Please point to the words as I read.* Then ask the child to finish reading the book while you record what the child reads on the Oral Reading Record. Note if the child uses picture cues effectively.
	KCR. 4 Identifies question mark and gives purpose.	Open to pages 8 and 9 and ask the child to point to a question mark. Ask: *What does a question mark do? What does it tell us about a sentence?*
	KCR. 5 Counts words in sentence.	Ask the child to count the number of words in the sentence on page 9.
	KCR. 6 Counts letters in words.	On that same page, point to the word *fish*. Ask the child to count the letters in the word.
	KCR. 7 Tells details of book.	Finally, close the book and ask the child to talk about the fish in the book. Say: *What was your favorite fish? What other kinds of fish did you read about?*

Segmenting	Assessment	Directions
Grouping: Small group or individual **Timeframe:** 15 minutes per student/group **Materials:** • Segmentation: Sentences to Words, p. 78 • Segmentation: Words to Syllables, p. 79 • Segmenting/Writing/ Letters Rubric, p. 76	KCS. 8 Segments words in sentences.	See the Segmentation: Sentences to Words (p. 78) for details.
	KCS. 9 Segments syllables in words.	See the Segmentation: Words to Syllables (p. 79) for details.

36 Week Assessment (cont.)

Note: You will need the Individual Student Profile (p. 61) for all assessments.

Writing	Assessment	Directions
Grouping: Small group **Timeframe:** 15 minutes **Materials:** • Stationery B, p. 195	KCW. 10 Draws picture to convey meaning. KCW. 11 Writes letters to make words about picture.	Give children copies of p. 195 and say, *Please draw a picture of a pet you have or would like to have. Then write about what you draw on the lines below.*

Letters	Assessment	Directions
Grouping: Individual **Timeframe:** 10 minutes per student **Materials:** • Letter Recognition Presentation Sheet, p. 198 • Letter Recognition Scoring Sheet, p. 197	KCW. 12 Identifies letters.	Show the child the Letter Recognition Sheet. Say: *Tell me the letters on this sheet.*
Grouping: Small group **Timeframe:** 15 minutes **Materials:** • Writing the Alphabet, p. 200 • Writing the Alphabet Teacher Directions, p. 199	KCW. 13 Writes letters.	Give letter writing boxes sheets to children and ask them to write letters. Say: *I will say a letter. Write the upper- and lowercase letter (big and small letter) in one box. Let's try the first one.* [Point to first box.] *Write the upper- and lowercase c in this box.* Continue in the same manner for the rest of the letters.

Reading **R**ubric

Task	4	3	2	I
KCR.I Finds title.	Turns over book and points to title without support.	Turns over book and points to title without support.	Needs support to find front and title.	Does not find title.
KCR.2 Understands directionality/voice-print match.	Points to print on page when reading and goes from one page to another.	Points to print on page when reading and goes from one page to another.	Gets confused from page to page and voice print match is not demonstrated.	Does not point to print.
KCR.3 Reads fluently.	0 to I error on words while reading.	2 errors on words while reading.	3 to 4 errors on words while reading.	More than 4 errors while reading.
KCR.4 Identifies question mark with purpose.	Readily points to question mark and says it tells you someone is asking you something.	Able to identify question mark but cannot give purpose or says the opposite.	Not able to identify question mark.	Not able to identify question mark.
KCR.5 Counts words in sentence.	Counts accurately.	Counts accurately.	Counts inaccurately but is off by I word only; i.e., says 5 words.	No response or very incorrect.
KCR.6 Counts letters in word.	Counts accurately.	Counts accurately.	Counts inaccurately but is off by I letter only.	No response or very incorrect.
KCR.7 Tells details of book.	Relates 3 or more adjectives about fish.	Relates 2 adjectives about fish.	Relates I adjective about fish.	No response.

Segmenting/Writing/Letters Rubric

Task	4	3	2	1
KCS.8 Segments words in sentences.	All correct.	4 correct out of 5 sentences.	3 correct out of 5 sentences.	Fewer than 3 correct.
KCS.9 Segments syllables in words.	All correct.	4 correct out of 5 sentences.	3 correct out of 5 sentences.	Fewer than 3 correct.
KCW.10 Draws picture to convey meaning.	Picture has a great deal of detail which is relevant to topic.	Picture is relevant to topic and has some detail.	Picture is skimpy and has little detail.	No picture or irrelevant picture, or very sparse picture that is difficult to understand.
KCW.11 Writes letters to make words about picture.	Writes a simple "sentence" or more using clusters of letters to represent words.	Writes some (at least 3) clusters of letters to represent words and thoughts. Clusters are 2 or more letters.	Writes only 1 or 2 clusters of letters, may be only 1 letter to represent words.	No writing or a letter or two for writing.
KCW.12 Identifies letters.	Identifies over 50 letters.	Identifies 50 out of 52 letters.	Identifies 40–49 of 52 letters.	Identifies fewer than 40 letters.
KCW.13 Writes letters.	Writes more than 26 letters correctly (reversing letters is acceptable—see test sheet for scoring).	Writes 26 out of 52 letters correctly (reversing letters is acceptable—see test sheet for scoring).	Writes 19–25 out of 52 letters correctly (reversing letters is acceptable—see test sheet for scoring).	Writes fewer than 19 letters correctly.

Oral **R**eading **R**ecord

Name _____ Date _____

Directions: Ask the child to read the mini-book aloud; record any mistakes here. Put a check (✓) over words read correctly and circle words omitted. If a word is mispronounced or a substitution is made, write the incorrect word over the correct word. If you had to say the word for the child, write T above the word. If an error is repeated over and over again (such as reading *look* for *like* in every sentence), count it as *one error*. If the child says *look* for *like* on one page, reads *like* correctly on the next, and then reads *look* for *like* on another page, count each error. Record your observations about the child's reading behaviors in the comments box.

36 Week Book — *Fish* by Brenda M. Weaver

Text	Comments
Fish are little.	
Fish are big.	
Fish are round.	
Fish are spotted.	
Fish are long.	
Fish are striped.	
Fish are scary.	
What do fish do?	

Scoring Guide
Orally read with 0–1 errors = 4; 2 errors = 3; 3–4 errors = 2; more than 4 errors = 1.

Segmentation: Sentences to Words

Name _____ Date _____

Directions: Gather a set of blocks (15 or so) or small items and place them on the desk or table where the child is seated. Tell the child that you will read a sentence aloud. Then ask the child to repeat the sentence and move one block out for each word he or she says. It is important for the child to say aloud the words as he or she segments the sentences so you can appropriately score the response; see the scoring guide below. It is acceptable for the child to move one block per word or per syllable. However, the child must at least correctly segment by words. You may repeat the sentence if there was some sort of interference, such as noise or talking, that distracted the student. You can use the practice items to model the task. Record scores on the Individual Student Profile.

Scoring Guide for Sentence Segmentation

Give one point for each correctly segmented sentence with no errors; put a check next to each correct sentence. Put a 0 for a sentence with any errors. The possible number of blocks is in parentheses after the sentence. If a child makes an error on one sentence, present the corresponding retest sentence. If the child segments the retest sentence correctly, award a point and disregard the error on the initial sentence.

Count each of the following as one error:

- Child cannot remember the sentence.
- Child uses one block for two words. For example, if the child says *like* and moves two blocks, it is one error.
- Child omits a word or words.

The following are not counted as errors:

- Child substitutes a word in the sentence but moves a block for it. For example, if you say *Tim ran* and the child repeats, *Tim swam* and moves two blocks, there are no errors.
- Child moves blocks by syllable. For example, in *Today is Sunday*, if a child moves two blocks for /sun/ and /day/, do not count it as an error. But if a child moves two blocks for *is*, do count it as an error.

Practice Sentences

_____ **Squirrels like to hunt for food.**

_____ **Today we will visit my grandpa.**

Test Sentences

1. _____ Harvey will get the card game. (6–7)
2. _____ We will get together to play store. (7–9)
3. _____ Pat is ready to play ball with me. (8–9)
4. _____ Let's go to the movies and eat popcorn. (8–10)
5. _____ Tomorrow we can play ball behind the school. (9–11)

Retest Sentences

1. _____ I like to eat red apples. (6–7)
2. _____ Today is my sister's birthday party. (6–10)
3. _____ Every year Sue marches in the holiday parade. (8–13)
4. _____ Can we buy a new car for my brother? (9–10)
5. _____ All of my friends like to eat pizza for lunch. (10–11)

Scoring: 5 correct out of 5 = 4; 4 correct out of 5 = 3; 3 correct out of 5 = 2; fewer than 3 correct = 1

Segmentation: Words to Syllables

Name _____ Date _____

Directions: Gather a set of blocks (5 or so) or small items for the child to use for segmenting words and place them on the desk or table where the child is seated. Tell the child that you will read a word aloud. Ask the child to repeat the word and move one block out for each syllable in the word. It is important for the child to say aloud the words as they are segmented so you can appropriately score the responses. You may repeat the word if there was some sort of interference, such as noise or talking, that distracted the child. You can use the practice items to model the task. Record scores on the Individual Student Profile.

Scoring Guide for Word Segmentation Task

Give one point for each correctly segmented word. If a child cannot segment a word into syllables, mark the item with a 0. The possible number of blocks is given in parentheses after each word.

Practice Words

_____ happy (2)

_____ doghouse (2)

_____ tomorrow (3)

Assessment Words

1. _____ properly (3)

2. _____ careless (2)

3. _____ monster (2)

4. _____ together (3)

5. _____ purple (2)

Scoring: 5 correct out of 5 = 4; 4 correct out of 5 = 3; 3 correct out of 5 = 2; fewer than 3 correct = 1

Grade 1 Assessments

Grade 1 is the year we hope that all students become independent readers who love books. The grade 1 assessments provided here help you evaluate students' skills in handling books, using cueing strategies, developing vocabulary, reading fluently, comprehending text, and writing—all essential skills for students to master on their way to becoming proficient readers. Students cement their knowledge of book-handling concepts this year and complete their understanding of the alphabet and language segmentation.

The major focuses of instruction during this critical year include cueing strategies, vocabulary development, and oral reading fluency. Students learn to use picture cues, semantics or meaning cues, syntax or sentence structure cues, and grapho-phonics or sound-symbol cues. To help students develop the use of these cues, it is essential to choose just the right text to appropriately support and challenge them. Vocabulary development is key in learning to read. Students must develop a significant sight vocabulary, words read immediately without decoding. Students also need to develop their awareness of word meanings and how words are used in sentences. Chapter 10 discusses various activities and techniques that can be used to instruct in these areas.

Basic, literal comprehension and writing skills begin to develop in grade 1 and are, therefore, assessed. Students learn to write words they know, to write down the sounds they hear in less familiar words, and to write messages. In first grade it is important for the students to understand that getting meaning from what they read and writing to communicate are the priorities.

There are three grade 1 assessments: A, B, and C. There is also a guide to Diagnostic Placement Tests at the beginning of the assessments to help you place students in reading levels and to determine their strengths and weaknesses. Each book used in the assessment is somewhat more difficult to read, thereby assessing more difficult learned competencies. Here is a chart showing the comparisons of the reading difficulty levels of the assessment books for grade 1:

Approximate Reading Levels for Grade 1 Assessment Books

Assessment	Weaver Literacy Levels	Guided Reading Levels*	Schulman & Payne Levels	Reading Recovery Levels	Traditional Basal Levels
Grade 1 Diagnostic Placement	Emergent B (EmB)	B–C	Emergent	2–3	Readiness
12th Week or 1AR	Early 1 A (E1A)	C–D	Progressing	4–5	Preprimer
24th Week or 1BR	Early 2 B (E2B)	E–F	Progressing	8–9	Preprimer
36th Week or 1CR	Early 3 (E3)	G–I	Progressing	10–11	Preprimer

Note: These are approximate levels due to the variety of leveling systems and the inability to have direct relationships between the leveling systems.

* Guided Reading Levels as described by Fountas and Pinnell in *Guided Reading* (1996).

The average first grader who is progressing at an average rate will score at the 3 level on each task for each assessment. Students scoring at the 4 level will need to be challenged in instruction, while those students scoring in the 1 to 2 range need intervention and retesting on those items in order to ensure adequate development. The intervention area is listed on the Individual Student Profile, and you'll find appropriate techniques and activities to address specific needs in the designated intervention chapter.

The Scoring Sheets

You will find two types of scoring sheets to help you make the most of the data you collect with the assessments. There is a grade 1 Individual Student Profile, on which you record specific information about individual students. This format allows you to see their growth over the course of a year. In addition, you will find a Class Record Sheet in the Appendix. I recommend preparing one of these for your class; it will summarize the class' performance, giving you an at-a-glance view of their overall weaknesses and strengths. In addition, the RTI Benchmark Chart will recommend the adjustments in instruction or support necessary at this time. Using these sheets will help you plan appropriate instruction for your reading groups.

A note about the assessments: Each item to be assessed is given a label for ease of reference. The first character indicates the grade level; for the first grade assessments, all assessment items begin with 1. The second

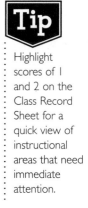

Tip

Highlight scores of 1 and 2 on the Class Record Sheet for a quick view of instructional areas that need immediate attention.

character indicates which assessment it belongs to (A, B, or C, meaning the 12 Week, 24 Week, and 36 Week Assessment, respectively) and the third character references the assessment area. For instance, 1AR indicates an item from the Grade 1 A Assessment that evaluates a reading skill. In addition, each item within an assessment area is then numbered to differentiate the tasks. In the Grade 1 A Assessment, there are seven items that assess reading skills, and they are numbered 1AR.1–1AR.7. In each assessment, the tasks are numbered this way, and the rubrics, scoring guides, and record sheets use the same labeling system.

Diagnostic Placement Tests for Students Entering During School Year

Time of School Year	Diagnostic Placement Test to Use	Comments
Weeks 1–11	Kindergarten C Assessment	If most areas are too difficult for student, the Kindergarten B Assessment can be given.
Weeks 13–23	Grade 1 A Assessment	Assessment items KCS.8 and KCS.9 on segmenting as well as KCW.12 and KCW.13 on letters should be given.
Weeks 25–35	Grade 1 B Assessment	Assessment items IAS.8 and IAS.9 on consonants should be given.
Week 37 to end of school year	Grade 1 C Assessment	Assessment items IBR.5 on vocabulary, IBS.6 on blends and digraphs, and IBS.7 on sound segmenting should and be given.

Individual Student Profile: Grade 1

Student: _____

Teacher: _____

12 Week Assessment

Area	Rubric Score	Intervention Area	Date
1AR.1 Points to the title.		Print Conventions: Book Familiarity	
1AR.2 Orally reads text using strategies.		Word Recognition: Cueing Strategies	
1AR.3 Points to three words when given by teacher.		Print Conventions: Text Concepts	
1AR.4 Isolates one and two letters and words in print.		Print Conventions: Text Concepts	
1AR.5 Completes a cloze exercise.		Comprehension: Cloze; Fiction Text	
1AR.6 Identifies and explains use of question mark and exclamation point.		Print Conventions: Text Features	
1AR.7 Identifies words from similar words when said by teacher.		Word Recognition: Visual Cueing Strategy	
1AS.8 Identifies initial consonants in words.		Word Recognition: Phonics	
1AS.9 Identifies final consonants in words.		Word Recognition: Phonics	
1AW.10 Writes letters of alphabet.		Writing: Alphabet	
1AW.11 Writes some response sentences.		Writing: Response; Mechanics	

Individual Student Profile: Grade 1

Student: _____

Teacher: _____

24 Week Assessment

Area	Rubric Score	Intervention Area	Date
1BR.1 Orally reads text using strategies.		Word Recognition: Cueing Strategies	
1BR.2 Orally retells story.		Comprehension: Retelling/Summarize; Fiction Text	
1BR.3 Identifies and explains the use of comma and quotation marks.		Print Conventions: Text Features	
1BR.4 Completes a cloze exercise.		Comprehension: Cloze	
1BR.5 Reads familiar sight vocabulary words.		Word Recognition: Word Study	
1BS.6 Identifies initial blends and digraphs in words.		Word Recognition: Phonics	
1BS.7 Segments sounds in words.		Word Recognition: Segmentation	
1BW.8 Writes a simple story.		Writing: Story; Mechanics	

Individual Student Profile: Grade 1

Student: _____

Teacher: _____

36 Week Assessment

Area	Rubric Score	Intervention Area	Date
1CR.1 Orally reads text using strategies.		Word Recognition: Cueing Strategies	
1CR.2 Retells book in writing.		Comprehension: Retelling/Summarizing; Fiction Text Writing: Mechanics	
1CR.3 Completes a cloze exercise.		Comprehension: Cloze	
1CS.4 Pronounces words with vowel patterns		Word Recognition: Phonics	
1CS.5 Identifies words from which contractions are made.		Word Recognition: Word Study	
1CS.6 Identifies appropriate word ending for sentences.		Word Recognition: Word Study	
1CW.7 Writes a response which has a minimum of five sentences.		Writing: Response; Mechanics	

RTI Benchmark Charts: Grade 1

12 Week

- Adequate Progress = Continue with present program
- Adjust Instruction = More small-group instruction with different materials/methods are necessary
- Outside Support = Student requires additional evaluation by support personnel and possible testing

Adequate Progress	Adjust Instruction	Outside Support
One or two items scored at 2 or below	Two of the following scored at 2 or below: 1AR.2, 1AR.5, 1AW.10, 1AW.11 AND one or more of the other items scored at 2 or below	All of the following scored at 2 or below: 1AR.2, 1AR.5, 1AW.10, 1AW.11 AND one or more of the other items scored at 2 or below

24 Week

- Adequate Progress = Continue with present program
- Adjust Instruction = More small-group instruction with different materials/methods are necessary
- Outside Support = Student requires additional evaluation by support personnel and possible testing

Adequate Progress	Adjust Instruction	Outside Support
One or two items scored at 2 or below	Two to four of the following items scored at 2 or below: 1BR.1, 1BR.4, 1BR.5, 1BS.7, 1BW.8 AND one or more of the other items scored at 2 or below	All of the following scored at 2 or below: 1BR.1, 1BR.4, 1BR.5, 1BS.7, 1BW.8 AND one or more of the other items scored at 2 or below

36 Week

- Adequate Progress = Continue with present program
- Adjust Instruction = More small-group instruction with different materials/methods are necessary
- Outside Support = Student requires additional evaluation by support personnel and possible testing

Adequate Progress	Adjust Instruction	Outside Support
One or two items scored at 2 or below	Two to four of the following scored at 2 or below: 1CR.1, 1CR.2, 1CR.3, 1CS.4, 1CW.7 AND one or more of the other items scored at 2 or below	All of the following scored at 2 or below: 1CR.1, 1CR.2, 1CR.3, 1CS.4, 1CW.7 AND one or more of the other items scored at 2 or below

Grade 1 A Assessment

12 Week Assessment

Note: You will need the Individual Student Profile (p. 83) and the Class Record Sheet (p. 193) for all assessments.

Reading	Assessment Areas	Directions
Grouping: Individual **Timeframe:** 20 minutes per student; cloze and identifying words can be done in a group setting if desired **Materials:** • *Little Bug, Little Bug,* by Brenda M. Weaver; see Appendix • Reading Rubric, p. 89 • Oral Reading Record, p. 91 • Cloze Exercise, p. 92 • Word Identification sheet, p. 93	1AR.1 Points to the title.	Give book to the child with its cover facing down. Say: *Please find the front of the book. Point to the title.* Read the title; then ask the child to read it.
	1AR.2 Orally reads text using strategies.	Say: *This book is about a little bug who is lost. Let's look at the pictures to see if the bug is found.* Open to the first page and do a picture walk by discussing each page, naming the places the bug might be hiding. Next, ask the child to return to the first page and begin reading. Write responses on the Oral Reading Record.
	1AR.3 Points to three words when given by teacher.	When the child finishes reading, turn to page 3 and ask the child to point to the words *under, you,* and *bed.*
	1AR.4 Isolates one and two letters and words in print.	Then open to page 6 and ask the child to point to one word, two words, one letter, and two letters (use *where* for the word in which to point to letters). Say: *Can you point to one word on this page for me? How about showing me two words? Great. Look at this word* (point to *where*). *Can you point to one letter in this word? How about two letters?*
	1AR.5 Completes a cloze exercise.	Then distribute the cloze sheet. Ask the child to write the word that makes sense using the story. (Student is **not** given book to use.)
	1AR.6 Identifies and explains use of question mark and exclamation point.	After student completes the sentences, ask the child to read them aloud. Then ask the child to point to the question mark. Ask: *Why do writers use questions marks?*
	1AR.7 Identifies words from similar words when said by teacher.	Give the child the Word Identification sheet. Each box contains four words. Tell the child you will read one word per box and ask the child to circle the word you say. Words to read: 1. little, 2. where, 3. bug, 4. rug, 5. here, 6. you.

Grade 1 A Assessment (cont.)

Note: Individual Student Profile (p. 83) and the Class Record Sheet (p. 193) are needed for all assessments.

Consonants	Assessment Areas	Directions
Grouping: Small group **Timeframe:** 10 minutes per task **Materials:** • Skills/Writing Rubric, p. 90 • Initial and Final Consonants assessment sheet, p. 94	1AS.8 Identifies initial consonants in words.	Distribute Initial and Final Consonants assessment sheets. Say: *I am going to read a word, and I want you to listen carefully for the beginning sound. Then circle the letter in the box that matches the sound. We'll do the first one together.* Say target words (listed below) without emphasizing consonants. **Initial consonants target words:** *ball, foot, mother, sat, roof, pat, run, down, wet, note, house, lamb, kite, cabbage, garage, vet, you, jump, zoo*
	1AS.9 Identifies final consonants in words.	Repeat the process described for initial consonants for final consonants. **Final consonants target words:** *bib, roof, dim, hill, hit, sip, car, load, hike, torn*

Writing/Letter	Assessment Areas	Directions
Grouping: Small group **Timeframe:** 15 minutes **Materials:** • Writing the Alphabet, p. 200 • Writing the Alphabet Teacher Directions, p. 199 • Stationery B, p. 195	1AW.10 Writes letters of alphabet.	Give Writing the Alphabet sheets to children and ask them to write letters. Say: *I will say a letter. Write the upper- and lowercase letter (big and small letter) in one box. Let's try the first one.* [Point to first box.] *Write the upper- and lowercase c in this box.* Continue in the same manner for the rest of the letters.
	1AW.11 Writes some response sentences.	Distribute stationery and say: *What is your favorite thing in your room? Draw a picture of it and then write sentences about what you do with it.*

Reading Rubric

Task	4	3	2	I
IAR.I Points to the title.	Turns over book and points to title without support.	Turns over book and points to title without support.	Needs support to find front and title.	Does not find title.
IAR.2 Orally reads text using strategies.	0 to 2 errors on words while reading.	3 errors on words while reading.	4 to 5 errors on words while reading.	More than 5 errors while reading.
IAR.3 Points to 3 words when given by teacher.	Readily points to 3 words when given by the teacher.	Points to 2 words given by the teacher.	Points to I word given by the teacher.	Points to no words correctly.
IAR.4 Isolates I and 2 letters and words in print.	Isolates I and 2 letters in a word; isolates I and 2 words in text.	Isolates I or 2 letters in a word; isolates I or 2 words in text; any combination as long as 3 out of 4 are correct.	Isolates I or 2 letters in a word; isolates I or 2 words in text; any combination as long as 2 out of 4 are correct.	Isolates I or 2 letters in a word; isolates I or 2 words in text; any combination as long as 0–I out of 4 are correct.
IAR.5 Completes a cloze exercise.	3 correct sentences; can use inventive spelling.	2 correct sentences; can use inventive spelling.	I correct sentence; can use inventive spelling.	0 correct sentences; can use inventive spelling.
IAR.6 Identifies and explains use of question mark and exclamation point.	Identification and use are counted separately; 4 correct total of identifications and uses (question mark—asks a question; exclamation mark—shows emotion, excitement, loud speech).	Identification and use are counted separately; 3 correct total of identifications and uses.	Identification and use are counted separately; 2 correct total of identifications and uses.	Identification and use are counted separately; fewer than 2 correct.
IAR.7 Identifies words from similar words when said by teacher.	6 correctly identified by student.	5 correctly identified by student.	3 or 4 correctly identified by student.	Fewer than 3 correctly identified by student.

Skills/Writing Rubric

Task	4	3	2	1
1AS.8 Identifies initial consonants in words.	Identifies 19 consonants correctly out of 19.	Identifies 17 or 18 consonants correctly out of 19.	Identifies 15 or 16 consonants correctly out of 19.	Identifies fewer than 15 consonants correctly out of 19.
1AS.9 Identifies final consonants in words.	Identifies 10 consonants correctly out of 10.	Identifies 9 consonants correctly out of 10.	Identifies 7 or 8 consonants correctly out of 10.	Identifies fewer than 7 consonants correctly out of 10.
1AW.10 Writes letters of the alphabet.	Writes 52 letters correctly (reversing letters is acceptable —see test sheet for scoring, p. 51.)	Writes 50 out of 52 letters correctly (reversing letters is acceptable —see test sheet for scoring, p. 51.)	Writes 45–49 out of 52 letters correctly (reversing letters is acceptable—see test sheet for scoring, p. 51.)	Writes fewer than 45 letters correctly.
1AW.11 Writes some response sentences.	Writes more than 2 simple sentences about room; inventive spelling is acceptable.	Writes 2 simple sentences about room; inventive spelling is acceptable.	Writes one simple sentence about room; inventive spelling is acceptable.	No writing or 1 or 2 letters or clusters of letters, not sentences.

Oral Reading Record

Name _____ Date _____

Directions: Ask the child to read the mini-book aloud; record any mistakes here. Put a check (✓) over words read correctly and circle words omitted. If a word is mispronounced or a substitution is made, write the incorrect word over the correct word. If you had to say the word for the child, write T above the word. If an error is repeated over and over again (such as reading *look* for *like* in every sentence), count it as *one error*. If the child says *look* for *like* on one page, reads *like* correctly on the next, and then reads *look* for *like* on another page, count each error. Record your observations about the child's reading behaviors in the comments box.

12 Week Book — *Little Bug, Little Bug* by Brenda M. Weaver

Text	Comments
Little bug, little bug, where are you?	
Are you under the bed?	
Little bug, little bug, where are you?	
Are you under the rug?	
Little bug, little bug, where are you?	
Are you in the box?	
Here you are, little bug!	

Scoring Guide
Orally read with 0–2 errors = 4; 3 errors = 3; 4–5 errors = 2; more than 5 errors = 1.

Cloze Exercise

Name _____ Date _____

Directions: Read the following sentences to yourself. They are about the book you just read. Fill in the blanks with a word which makes sense from the story.

1. Are you under the _____ ?

2. Here you are, little _____ !

3. Little bug, little bug, where are _____ ?

Word **I**dentification

Name _____ Date _____

Directions: Your teacher will read one word for each box. Find the word and circle it.

❶

like
little
love
let

❷

where
what
who
went

❸

bed
bet
bug
bat

❹

rat
rug
running
rake

❺

Hit
Help
Here
Have

❻

yet
young
yes
you

Scoring: 6 correct = 4; 5 correct = 3; 3–4 correct =2; less than 3 correct =1

Initial Consonants

Name _____   Date _____

m b	f s	m f	s l	t r
p s	y r	w d	m w	n v
p h	w l	k b	c l	b g
v y	m y	j h	z p	

Final Consonants

m b	f s	m f	s l	t r
p s	y r	w d	m k	n v

Grade 1 B Assessment

24 Week Assessment

Note: Individual Student Profile (p. 84) and Class Record Sheet (p. 193) are needed for all assessments.

Reading	Assessment Areas	Directions
Grouping: Individual **Timeframe:** 15 minutes per student **Materials:** • *My Cat Is Lost* by Brenda M. Weaver; see Appendix • Reading Rubric, p. 97 • Oral Reading Record, p. 98 • Oral Retelling Form, p. 99	1BR.1 Orally reads text using strategies.	Give book to the child. Show the child the cover and say: *Let's read the title together.* Read title with the child and then say: *This book is about a cat that is lost. Where might a cat hide? Let's look at the pictures to see what happens.* Open the book to the first page and do a picture walk by turning the pages and allowing the child to describe what is happening. Next, ask the child to return to the first page and begin reading. Take an oral reading record.
	1BR.2 Orally retells story.	After the child has completed the book, ask the child to retell the story in his or her own words.
Grouping: Individual **Timeframe:** 10 minutes for cloze; 5 minutes for sight words **Materials:** • Reading Rubric, p. 97 • Sentence and Cloze Exercise sheet, p. 100 • Sight word flashcards (teacher prepared; see directions at right) • Sight Vocabulary Recording Sheet, p. 101	1BR.3 Identifies and explains the use of comma and quotation marks.	Give the child the Sentence and Cloze Exercise sheet and ask the child to look at the first sentence on the sheet. Read the sentence aloud. Then say: *Please point to the comma in the sentence. What is the job of a comma? Can you point to the quotation mark for me? Why do writers use quotation marks?*
	1BR.4 Completes a cloze exercise.	Ask child to complete the cloze portion of the sheet. Say: *Please read these sentences from the story and fill in the blanks with words that make sense.* (Student is **not** given book to use.)
	1BR.5 Reads familiar sight vocabulary words.	Put vocabulary words on individual index cards. The student reads the words on the cards; record the answers on the appropriate sheet. Say: *Read these words for me. Try to say them quickly without sounding them out.* Words are to be said without sounding them out. **Words for sight word flashcards:** *where, are, very, away, every, next, here, about, no, down, there, with, have, you, goes*

24 Week Assessment (cont.)

Note: Individual Student Profile (p. 84) and Class Record Sheet (p. 193) needed for all assessments.

Skills	Assessment Areas	Directions
Grouping: Whole group **Timeframe:** 10 minutes **Materials:** • Blends and Digraphs worksheet, p. 102	1BS.6 Identifies initial blends and digraphs in words.	Distribute Blends and Digraphs worksheets. Say: *I'm going to read some words, and I want you to listen for the beginning sounds. Write the beginning sounds that you hear on the worksheet.* Say the words without emphasizing the initial blends or digraphs. **Blends and digraphs words:** *bring, spill, shake, chip, what, clap, thank, crash, small, swat, quake, skate, glad, frog, dress*
Grouping: Individual **Timeframe:** 10 minutes per student **Materials:** • Segmentation: Sounds assessment sheet, p. 103 • Set of 5 markers or other small items	1BS.7 Segments sounds in words.	See the Segmentation: Sounds assessment sheet (p. 103) for details.

Writing	Assessment Areas	Directions
Grouping: Whole group **Timeframe:** 15 minutes **Materials:** • Writing Rubric, p. 97 • Stationery B, p. 195	1BW.8 Writes a simple story.	Distribute writing stationery and say: *Let's think about all the things we like to do outside. There are so many things I like to do.* [name some] *I'd like you to write a short story about something you like to do outdoors. You can draw a picture of it first. Then write what it is, how you do it, and where you do it. Use additional writing sheets if you need them. Please put in the appropriate capitals, punctuation, and spelling that you know.* Also write the prompt on the board or chart paper.

Reading/Skills Rubric

Task	4	3	2	1
1BR.1 Orally reads text using strategies.	0 to 3 errors on words while reading.	4 errors on words while reading.	5 errors on words while reading.	More than 5 errors while reading.
1BR.2 Orally retells story.	Retells story with a beginning, middle, and end of the main events.	Retells story with a beginning, middle, and end but also gives extra details of story.	Retells two of the three: beginning, middle, and end of main events.	Retells one or none of: beginning, middle, and end of main events.
1BR.3 Identifies and explains the use of comma and quotation marks (comma tells us to pause; quotes show someone talking).	Identification and use are counted separately; 4 correct total out of 4 total identifications and uses.	Identification and use are counted separately; 3 correct total out of 4 total of identifications and uses.	Identification and use are counted separately; 2 correct total out of 4 total of identifications and uses.	Identification and use are counted separately; fewer than 2 correct total out of 4 total of identifications and uses.
1BR.4 Completes a cloze exercise.	5 correct sentences; can use inventive spelling.	4 correct sentences; can use inventive spelling.	2 or 3 correct sentences; can use inventive spelling.	0 or 1 correct sentence; can use inventive spelling.
1BR.5 Reads familiar sight vocabulary words.	Reads 15 out of 15 words correctly and quickly without sounding out.	Reads 14 out of 15 words correctly and quickly with very little sounding out.	Slowly reads 10–13 out of 15 words correctly, sometimes sounding out.	Laboriously reads fewer than 10 words correctly; sounds out all words.
1BS.6 Identifies initial blends and digraphs in words.	Identifies 14–15 out of 15 correctly.	Identifies 13 out of 15 correctly.	Identifies 10–12 out of 15 correctly.	Identifies fewer than 10 correctly.
1BS.7 Segments sounds in words.	Segments 17–18 out of 18 words correctly.	Segments 16 out of 18 words correctly.	Segments 12–15 out of 18 words correctly.	Segments fewer than 12 words correctly.

Writing Rubric

Task	4	3	2	1
1BW.8 Writes a simple story.	Writes more than 5 sentences. Sentences are correctly written for grammar and content. Most of the words are conventional spellings. Story has a beginning and end with several details.	Writes 4 or 5 sentences. Sentences are correctly written for grammar and content. Many of the words are conventional spellings, but some are inventive spellings. Story has a beginning and end with some details.	Writes 3 or 4 sentences. Sentences are simple and not always correct for grammar and content. Many of the words are inventive spellings. Story has a beginning or an end with few details.	Writes fewer than 3 sentences which are poorly constructed. Words are difficult to read due to poor spellings. Story does not seem to have a beginning or end and no details.

Oral Reading Record

Name _____ Date _____

Directions: Ask the child to read the mini-book aloud; record any mistakes here. Put a check (✓) over words read correctly and circle words omitted. If a word is mispronounced or a substitution is made, write the incorrect word over the correct word. If you had to say the word for the student, write T above the word. If an error is repeated over and over again (such as reading *look* for *like* in every sentence), count it as *one error*. If the child says *look* for *like* on one page, reads *like* correctly on the next, and then reads *look* for *like* on another page, count each error. Record your observations about the child's reading behaviors in the comments box.

24 Week Book — *My Cat Is Lost* by Brenda M. Weaver

Text	Comments
Buffy is my cat.	
We play with a ball.	
I feed Buffy.	
One day, I can not find Buffy.	
I look in the kitchen. No Buffy.	
I look in my bedroom. No Buffy.	
I look in the closet.	
There's Buffy sleeping on the blanket.	

Scoring Guide
Orally read with 0–3 errors = 4; 4 errors = 3; 5 errors = 2; more than 5 errors = 1.

Oral Retelling Form

Name _____ Date _____

Directions: Ask the child to retell *My Cat Is Lost* in his or her own words. Remind the child to include the beginning, middle, and end and to tell only important details.

Retelling	Comments
Beginning: Buffy is a cat who belongs to a girl.	
Middle: One day, the girl cannot find Buffy. She looks in many places: the kitchen, the bedroom, and the closet.	
End: In the end, the girl finds Buffy on the blanket in the closet.	

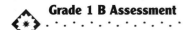

Sentence and Cloze Exercise

Name _____   Date _____

Sentence Exercise

"Quack," said the duck. "There's a bug on me."

Directions: Read the following sentences to yourself. They are about the book you just read. Fill in the blanks with a word which makes sense using the story. Your teacher will not be able to help you with any words.

1. We play with a _____ .

2. I _____ Buffy.

3. One day, I can not _____ Buffy.

4. I look in my _____ .

5. There's Buffy _____ on the blanket.

Scoring Guide

Answers: 1. ball, 2. feed, 3. find, 4. three acceptable answers: kitchen, closet, bedroom, 5. sleeping. If a word other than the one in the story is used, it can be given credit if it makes sense in the sentence and follows the story. For example: if a child writes, *I can not play with Buffy* for sentence 3, it is incorrect. But if the child writes, *I can not see Buffy*, it is acceptable because it fits the story and makes sense.

Scoring Key: 5 correct = 4; 4 correct = 3; 3–2 correct = 2; 1–0 correct = 1

Sight Vocabulary Recording Sheet

Name _____ Date _____

1. _____ where   6. _____ next   11. _____ there

2. _____ are   7. _____ here   12. _____ with

3. _____ very   8. _____ about   13. _____ have

4. _____ away   9. _____ no   14. _____ you

5. _____ every   10. _____ down   15. _____ goes

Scoring: Students need to say words rather quickly, without decoding. 15 correct out of 15 = 4; 14 correct out of 15 = 3; 10–13 correct out of 15 = 2; fewer than 10 correct = 1.

Blends and Digraphs

Name _____ Date _____

___ ing	___ ill	___ ake	___ ip	___ at
___ ap	___ ank	___ ash	___ all	___ at
___ ake	___ ate	___ ad	___ og	___ ess

Scoring Guide

14–15 correct out of 15 = 4; 13 correct out of 15 = 3; 10–12 correct out of 15 = 2; less than 10 correct = 1

Segmentation: **S**ounds

Name _____ Date _____

Directions: Gather a set of blocks (5 or so) or small items for the child to use for segmenting words and place them on the desk or table where the child is seated. Tell the child that you will read a word aloud. Ask the child to repeat the word and move one block out for each sound in the word. It is important for the child to say aloud the words as they are segmented so you can appropriately score the responses. You may repeat the word if there was some sort of interference, such as noise or talking, that distracted the child. You can use the practice items to model the task.

Scoring Guide for Word Segmentation Task

Give one point for each correctly segmented word. If a child cannot segment a word, mark the item with a 0. The correct number of blocks is given in parentheses after each word. Over segmentation is acceptable, then point out to the child that he or she needs to shorten the expanse of the word into sounds. For example, some children will attach a vowel-type sound to consonants, saying "H" as /h/ and /a/. Once this is pointed out to them, children will complete the rest of the test appropriately.

Practice Words

_____ go (2)

_____ flip (4)

_____ moat (3)

Test Words

1. _____ fad (3)	7. _____ met (3)	13. _____ mend (4)
2. _____ me (2)	8. _____ hike (3)	14. _____ fit (3)
3. _____ tip (3)	9. _____ so (2)	15. _____ sap (3)
4. _____ lot (3)	10. _____ clock (4)	16. _____ hi (2)
5. _____ rule (3)	11. _____ gut (3)	17. _____ flow (3)
6. _____ take (3)	12. _____ flake (4)	18. _____ seed (3)

Scoring Guide

17–18 correct out of 18 = 4; 16 correct out of 18 = 3; 12–15 correct out of 18 = 2; fewer than 12 correct = 1

Grade 1 C Assessment

36 Week Assessment

Note: Individual Student Profile (p. 85) and Class Record Sheet (p. 193) are needed for all assessments.

Reading	Assessment Areas	Directions
Grouping: Individual or in a group of 2 students **Timeframe:** 20 minutes for reading; 10 minutes for response; 10–15 minutes for cloze **Materials:** • *Frisco and Pippin Are Friends* by Brenda M. Weaver (see Appendix) • Reading Rubric, p. 106 • Oral Reading Record, pp. 107–108 • Written Retelling sheet, p. 109 • Cloze Exercise sheet, p. 110	1CR.1 Orally reads text using strategies.	Read the title together with the child(ren). Say: *This book is about two dogs who are friends: Frisco and Pippin. Do you have a dog? What kinds of things do dogs do?* [Discuss dog behaviors briefly.] *Let's look at the pictures to see what these two dogs do.* Open to the first page and quickly discuss the pictures. Then ask the child to read aloud. (If working with two readers, have the first reader do pages 2–7 and the second reader do pages 8–12.) Use the Oral Reading Record to record the reading. If only assessing one child, have him or her read pages 2–7 aloud, and then have the child finish reading the book silently. After the story has been read, present the Written Retelling and Cloze Exercise sheets for the student(s) to complete independently. Read the directions for each part and explain the tasks to the children. Do not offer support, and do not allow the book to be used.
	1CR.2 Retells book in writing. 1CR.3 Completes a cloze exercise.	When the child finishes reading, hand out the Written Retelling and Cloze Exercise sheets for the child to work on independently. Read the directions for each part aloud and explain the tasks, but do not offer support on completing the tasks. Children may not reference the book during the tasks.

36 Week Assessment (cont.)

Note: Individual Student Profile (p. 85) and Class Record Sheet (p. 193) are needed for all assessments.

Skills	Assessment Areas	Directions
Grouping: Individual **Timeframe:** 10 minutes **Materials:** • Word cards • Vowel Patterns sheet, p. 111	1CS.4 Pronounces words with vowel patterns (short/long/r-controlled patterns).	Make word cards for the list of vowel pattern words, shown on p. 111. Present word cards to the student and ask him or her to read them. The student's response is recorded on the Vowel Patterns sheet.
Grouping: Whole group **Timeframe:** 10 minutes **Materials:** • Contractions and Endings worksheet, p. 112	1CS.5 Identifies words from which contractions are made. 1CS.6 Identifies appropriate word ending for sentences.	Distribute Contractions and Endings worksheets to the group. Read the directions aloud and ask students to complete the tasks independently.

Writing	Assessment Areas	Directions
Grouping: Whole or small group **Timeframe:** 15 minutes **Materials:** • Stationery B, p. 195	1CW.7 Writes a response with a minimum of 5 sentences.	Distribute Stationery B to students. Say: *We've all read* Frisco and Pippin are Friends, *a funny story about two dogs. I'd like you to think about what kind of animal you would like to have as a pet. It can be a pet you have now, or one you would like to have someday. Tell what kind of animal it is and what it can do. What kinds of things would you do with it? What does it eat and where does it sleep?* Discuss one example from students. Write the prompt on the board as well: Pets—What kind do I have or want to have? What can it do? What would I do with it? What does it eat? Where does it sleep?

Reading Rubric

Task	4	3	2	1
1CR.1 Orally reads text using strategies.	0 to 4 errors on words while reading.	5 to 8 errors on words while reading.	9 to 11 errors on words while reading.	More than 11 errors while reading.
1CR.2 Retells book in writing.	All sentences relate to story and are a brief retelling of story.	All sentences relate to story and are almost a complete retelling of the story with a beginning, middle, and end.	Only some of the sentences relate to the story and it is not a complete retelling of the story.	Sentences not relevant to the story or completely irrelevant to story.
1CR.3 Completes a cloze exercise.	5 correct sentences; can use inventive spelling.	4 correct sentences; can use inventive spelling.	3 correct sentences; can use inventive spelling.	2 - 0 correct sentences; can use inventive spelling.

Skills Rubric

Task	4	3	2	1
1CS.4 Pronounces words with vowel patterns.	Correctly pronounces 20 out of 20 words.	Correctly pronounces 19 out of 20 words.	Correctly pronounces 15–18 out of 20 words.	Correctly pronounces fewer than 15 words.
1CS.5 Identifies words from which contractions are made.	Identifies 10 pairs of words correctly.	Identifies 8 or 9 pairs of words correctly.	Identifies 6 or 7 pairs of words correctly.	Identifies fewer than 6 pairs of words correctly.
1CS.6 Identifies appropriate word ending for sentences.	Identifies 5 words correctly for sentences.	Identifies 4 words correctly for sentences.	Identifies 2 or 3 words correctly for sentences.	Identifies 0 or 1 word correctly for sentences.

Writing Rubric

Task	4	3	2	1
1CW.7 Writes a response which has a minimum of 5 sentences.	Writes more than 5 sentences. Sentences are correctly written for grammar and content. Most of the words are conventional spellings. Response answers all questions with several details.	Writes 5 sentences. Sentences are correctly written for grammar and content. Most of the words are conventional spellings but some are inventive spellings. Response answers all questions with details.	Writes 3 or 4 sentences. Sentences are simple and not always correct for grammar and content. Many of the words are inventive spellings. Response answers some of the questions.	Writes fewer than 3 sentences which are poorly constructed. Words are difficult to read due to poor spellings. Response answers few to none of the questions.

Oral Reading Record

Frisco and Pippin Are Friends Part A

Name _____ Date _____

Directions: Ask the child to read the mini-book aloud; record any mistakes here. Put a check (✓) over words read correctly and circle words omitted. If a word is mispronounced or a substitution is made, write the incorrect word over the correct word. If you had to say the word for the student, write T above the word. If an error is repeated over and over again (such as reading *look* for *like* in every sentence), count it as *one error*. If the child says *look* for *like* on one page, reads *like* correctly on the next, and then reads *look* for *like* on another page, count each error. Record your observations about the child's reading behaviors in the comments box.

36 Week Book — *Frisco and Pippin Are Friends* by Brenda M. Weaver

Text	Comments
Frisco is a gray dog. He lives with Alicia.	
Pippin is a brown and white dog. She lives with Kayla. Alicia and Kayla are friends.	
One day Frisco sees Pippin playing next door.	
Frisco runs over to Pippin. They sniff noses and wag their tails. Then they begin to chase each other. They are having fun.	
Kayla calls, "Pippin, come. It's time for dinner." Alicia calls, "Frisco, come. Here's your food." Both dogs keep playing.	
Kayla runs to get Pippin. Alicia runs to get Frisco. Both dogs go home for dinner.	

Scoring Guide

Orally read with 0–4 errors = 4; 5–8 errors = 3; 9–11 errors = 2; more than 11 errors = 1.

Oral Reading Record

Frisco and Pippin Are Friends Part B

Name _____ Date _____

Directions: Ask the child to read the mini-book aloud; record any mistakes here. Put a check (✔) over words read correctly and circle words omitted. If a word is mispronounced or a substitution is made, write the incorrect word over the correct word. If you had to say the word for the student, write T above the word. If an error is repeated over and over again (such as reading *look* for *like* in every sentence), count it as *one error*. If the child says *look* for *like* on one page, reads *like* correctly on the next, and then reads *look* for *like* on another page, count each error. Record your observations about the child's reading behaviors in the comments box.

36 Week Book — *Frisco and Pippin Are Friends* by Brenda M. Weaver

Text	Comments
After eating, Pippin and Frisco play together in Pippin's yard. They see a squirrel on the bird feeder.	
The dogs run to the tree and bark at the squirrel. They bark until Alicia and Kayla call them.	
The next day, Alicia and Kayla go swimming. Pippin and Frisco go with them. The dogs jump in the pool. They splash and swim with the girls.	
When the dogs get tired, they jump out and shake the water off. The girls still play in the pool.	
Frisco and Pippin lie in the sun to dry off. Frisco and Pippin are great friends!	

Scoring Guide
Orally read with 0–4 errors = 4; 5–8 errors = 3; 9–11 errors = 2; more than 11 errors = 1.

Written **R**etelling

Name _____ Date _____

Reading Response

What was *Frisco and Pippin Are Friends* about? What happened in the story?
Try to tell what happened in the beginning and end of the story.

_____

- -

_____

- -

_____

- -

_____

- -

_____

- -

_____

- -

_____

Cloze Exercise

Name _____ Date _____

Directions: Read the following sentences to yourself. They are about the book you just read, *Frisco and Pippin Are Friends*. Fill in the blanks with a word from the story that makes sense.

1. They sniff noses and _____ their tails.

2. Alicia calls, "Frisco, come. Here's your _____ ."

3. Pippin and Frisco see a _____ on the bird feeder.

4. The next day, Alicia and Kayla go _____ .

5. Frisco and Pippin lie in the _____ to dry off.

Scoring Guide

Answers: 1. wag; 2. food; 3. squirrel; 4. swimming; 5. sun. Note: If a word other than the one in the story is used, the student can be given credit if the word makes sense in the sentence and follows the story. Example: for sentence 2, dinner or supper would also be appropriate to the story.

Scoring for cloze: 5 correct = 4; 4 correct = 3; 3 correct = 2; 2–0 correct = 1

Vowel Patterns

Name _____ Date _____

Directions: Have student read words off word cards; record their responses here. As long as the student sounds out the word or says the word correctly, mark it correct.

1. _____ hint

2. _____ blame

3. _____ rake

4. _____ rods

5. _____ meet

6. _____ surf

7. _____ hide

8. _____ sting

9. _____ stir

10. _____ snub

11. _____ check

12. _____ clove

13. _____ harder

14. _____ slices

15. _____ cape

16. _____ spokes

17. _____ sport

18. _____ haying

19. _____ mute

20. _____ scans

Scoring Guide

20 correct = 4; 19 correct = 3; 15–18 correct = 2; 14–0 correct = 1

Contractions and Endings

Name _____ Date _____

Contractions

Directions: Match the contractions with the words they stand for.

1. don't		I will
2. haven't		do not
3. won't		did not
4. can't		she would
5. didn't		will not
6. I'll		have not
7. she'd		I have
8. I've		could not
9. isn't		is not
10. couldn't		can not

> **Scoring Guide**
> 10 correct = 4; 8–9 correct = 3; 6–7 correct =2; 0–5 correct =1

Endings

Directions: Read these sentences and write in the blanks the best word to complete the sentence.

1. She likes _____ on the bed.   jumped jumping

2. The boy _____ up the road to the next town.   hiking hiked

3. The dog _____ to get in the house.   runs running

4. Mike is _____ the ball.   hits hitting

5. Cats like to _____ in the sand.   digging dig

> **Scoring Guide**
> 5 correct = 4; 4 correct = 3; 2-3 correct =2; 0-1 correct =1

Grade 2 Assessments

The grade 2 assessments cover cueing strategies, vocabulary development, oral fluency, comprehension, literary elements, and writing. Students are completing the strategies and skills in oral fluency and are learning to read most text silently. The emphasis is shifting from oral fluency to reading silently for comprehension.

The major focuses of instruction during this important year include cueing strategies, vocabulary development, and oral reading fluency. Students learn to integrate picture cues, semantics or meaning cues, syntax or sentence structure cues, and grapho-phonics or sound-symbol cues. To help students use these strategies efficiently and effectively, it is essential to choose just the right text to support and challenge them. Vocabulary development continues to be key. Students must develop a significant sight vocabulary, words read immediately without decoding. Students also need to develop their awareness of word meanings and how words are used in sentences. Chapter 10 discusses various activities and techniques that can be used to instruct in these areas.

In terms of comprehension, students are learning to interpret text and draw conclusions. They are learning to use what they read to learn new ideas. They are also becoming aware of the literary elements in narrative text. In writing, students are composing short stories and responding to what they read. They also write about things that they know.

There are three grade 2 assessments: A, B, and C. There is also a guide to Diagnostic Placement Tests at the beginning of the assessments to help you place students in reading levels and to determine their strengths and weaknesses. Each book used in the assessment is somewhat more difficult to read, thereby assessing more difficult learned competencies. Here is a chart showing the comparisons of the reading difficulty levels of the assessment books for grade 2:

Approximate Reading Levels for Grade 2 Assessment Books

Assessment	Weaver Literacy Levels	Guided Reading Levels*	Schulman & Payne Levels	Reading Recovery Levels	Traditional Basal Levels
12th Week or 2AR	Early 4 (E4)	I	Transitional	14–16	Grade 1
24th Week or 2BR	Fluency 1 (F1)	J–K	Fluent	17–18	Grade 2
36th Week or 2CR	Fluency 2 (F2)	L–M	Fluent	20–22	Grade 2

Note: These are approximate levels due to the variety of leveling systems and the inability to have direct relationships between the leveling systems.

* Guided Reading Levels as described by Fountas and Pinnell in *Guided Reading* (1996).

The average second grader who is progressing at an average rate will score at the 3 level on each task for each assessment. Students scoring at the 4 level will need to be challenged in instruction, while those students scoring in the 1 to 2 range need intervention and retesting on those items in order to ensure adequate development. The intervention area is listed on the Individual Student Profile, and you'll find appropriate techniques and activities to address specific needs in the designated intervention chapter.

The Scoring Sheets

You will find two types of scoring sheets to help you make the most of the data you collect with the assessments. There is a grade 2 Individual Student Profile, on which you record specific information about individual students. This format allows you to see their growth over the course of a year. In addition, you will find a Class Record Sheet in the Appendix. I recommend preparing one of these for your class; it will summarize the class' performance, giving you an at-a-glance view of their overall weaknesses and strengths. In addition, the RTI Benchmark Chart will recommend the adjustments in instruction or support necessary at this time. Using these sheets will help you plan appropriate instruction for your reading groups

Tip

Highlight scores of 1 and 2 on the Class Record Sheet for a quick view of instructional areas that need immediate attention.

A note about the assessments: Each item to be assessed is given a label for ease of reference. The first character indicates the grade level; for the second grade assessments, all assessment items begin with 2. The second character indicates which assessment it belongs to (A, B, or C, meaning the 12 Week, 24 Week, and 36 Week Assessment, respectively) and the third character references the assessment area.

For instance, 2AR indicates an item from the Grade 2 A Assessment that evaluates a reading skill. In addition, each item within an assessment area is then numbered to differentiate the tasks. In the Grade 2 A Assessment, there are two items that assess reading skills, and they are numbered 2AR.1–2AR.2. In each assessment, the tasks are numbered this way, and the rubrics, scoring guides, and record sheets use the same labeling system.

Diagnostic Placement Tests for Students Entering During School Year

Time of School Year	Diagnostic Placement Test to Use	Comments
Weeks 1–11	Grade 1 C Assessment	If most areas are too difficult for student, then Grade 1 B Assessment should be given. 1BS.7 on sound segmenting and 1BR.5 on reading sight vocabulary should also be given if giving Grade 1 C assessment.
Weeks 13–23	Grade 2 A Assessment	Assessment item 1BS.7 on sound segmenting should also be given.
Weeks 25–35	Grade 2 B Assessment	Assessment item 2AS.3 on pronouncing words with vowel patterns should be given. Also, an oral reading record of a few pages of the assessment book should be done. Students are allowed 1 error for every 10 words.
Week 37 to end of school year	Grade 2 C Assessment	If this assessment is too difficult for the student, then the Grade 2 B Assessment should be given. Also, an oral reading record of a few pages of the assessment book should be done. Students are allowed 1 error for every 10 words.

Individual Student Profile: Grade 2

Student: _____

Teacher: _____

12 Week Assessment

Area	Rubric Score	Intervention Area	Date
2AR.1 Orally reads text using strategies.		Word Recognition: Cueing Strategies	
2AR.2 Retells story in writing.		Comprehension: Retelling/Summarize; Fiction Text, Writing: Mechanics	
2AS.3 Pronounces words with vowel patterns.		Word Recognition: Phonics	
2AW.4 Writes a story which includes a beginning, middle, and end. Includes adjectives.		Writing: Story; Enhancement; Mechanics	

24 Week Assessment

Area	Rubric Score	Intervention Area	Date
2BR.1 Silently reads text and writes a brief summary.		Comprehension: Retelling/Summarize; Fiction Text, Writing: Mechanics	
2BR.2 Identifies problem of story and ways to solve problem.		Comprehension: Problem/Resolution Writing: Mechanics	
2BR.3 Completes a cloze exercise without book use.		Comprehension: Cloze	
2BS.4 Completes sentences using appropriate prefixes and suffixes.		Word Recognition: Word Study	
2BW.5 Writes a story with problem, steps for resolution, and a resolution.		Writing: Story; Mechanics; Genre	

36 Week Assessment

Area	Rubric Score	Intervention Area	Date
2CR.1 Silently reads text and responds to questions.		Comprehension: Detail; Finding Facts; Nonfiction Text Writing: Mechanics	
2CW.2 Writes a response to the question with appropriate supporting details from the text.		Writing: Response; Mechanics	

RTI Benchmark Charts: Grade 2

12 Week
- Adequate Progress = Continue with present program
- Adjust Instruction = More small-group instruction with different materials/methods are necessary
- Outside Support = Student requires additional evaluation by support personnel and possible testing

Adequate Progress	Adjust Instruction	Outside Support
No items should be scored at 2 or below	No more than two items scored at 2 or below	Three or more items scored at 2 or below

24 Week
- Adequate Progress = Continue with present program
- Adjust Instruction = More small-group instruction with different materials/methods are necessary
- Outside Support = Student requires additional evaluation by support personnel and possible testing

Adequate Progress	Adjust Instruction	Outside Support
No items should be scored at 2 or below	No more than two items scored at 2 or below	Three or more items scored at 2 or below

36 Week
- Adequate Progress = Continue with present program
- Adjust Instruction = More small-group instruction with different materials/methods are necessary
- Outside Support = Student requires additional evaluation by support personnel and possible testing

Adequate Progress	Adjust Instruction	Outside Support
No items should be scored at 2 or below	No more than one item scored at 2 or below	Both items scored at 2 or below

Grade 2 A Assessment

12 Week Assessment

Note: Individual Student Profile (p. 116) and Class Record Sheet (p. 193) needed for all assessments.

Reading	Assessment Areas	Directions
Grouping: Individual or in a group of 2 students **Timeframe:** 15 minutes **Materials:** • *The Mystery of the Missing Cat Food* by Betsy Franco; see Appendix • Reading Rubric, p. 119 • Oral Reading Record, p. 120–121 • Retelling Form, p. 122	2AR.1 Orally reads text using strategies.	Look at the cover with the child(ren). Say: *This book is a mystery. What is a mystery?* [Discuss.] *Let's read the title together aloud.* [Read title.] *What do you think the mystery is in this book? Now, open the book and for a minute or two go through the pictures to see what the clues are to solve the mystery.* [Discuss.] *Okay, let's read the story now.* Ask the children to read aloud and take an oral reading record. If one child is reading, have him or her stop at the end of page 6 and finish the story silently. If you are testing two students, the first student reads pages 2–7 and the second reads pages 8–12.
	2AR.2 Retells story in writing.	After the story has been read, have student(s) complete the Retelling Form independently. Read the directions aloud, but do not offer support during the task. Students may use the book only for looking up the spellings of words.

Skills	Assessment Areas	Directions
Grouping: Individual **Timeframe:** 5 minutes **Materials:** • Word cards (teacher-created; see directions at right) • Vowel Patterns Record Sheet, p. 123	2AS.3 Pronounces words with vowel patterns (double vowel patterns).	Make word cards for the list of nonsense words on p. 123. Show cards to the student and ask him or her to read them aloud, sounding them out using what they know about letters and the sounds they make. Record the response on the Vowel Patterns Record Sheet. **Words for word cards:** *fleet, reblewing, tweaker, smook, snoil, minpention, haudit, joast, preventure, maw, champoo, tounding, slown, mowler, squeating, glent*

Writing	Assessment Areas	Directions
Grouping: Small group **Timeframe:** 20 minutes per student **Materials:** • Blank, lined paper	2AW.4 Writes a story which includes a beginning, middle, and end.	Distribute writing sheets and say, *We just read a mystery about Joe and his sister finding out why the cat food was missing. Write your own story about an adventure you might have or someone else might have. It can be real or make believe. Be sure to include a beginning, middle, and end. Try to make the story descriptive with adjectives. Before you begin, you might want to try* [name some prewriting strategies you've worked on] *to get some ideas.*

Reading Rubric

Task	4	3	2	1
2AR.1 Orally reads text using strategies.	Reads fluently with expression. 0–5 errors.	Reads fluently. No more than 8–11 errors. Errors do not impact understanding.	Has fewer than 11 errors but reading is not fluent and a great deal of support is needed. **or** Has 12–15 errors; reading is not very fluent.	Reading is not fluent and has more than 15 errors.
2AR.2 Retells story in writing.	Retelling is complete with the beginning, middle, and end. The retelling includes problem, resolution, and all the clues: flour on floor, finds what footprints were made by, figures out size of dog, asks about dogs in neighborhood. Retelling has good sentence structure, mostly conventional spelling, and appropriate mechanics.	Retelling has beginning, middle, and end but does not include all the clues (must have at least 3 clues). Retelling has appropriate sentence structure, conventional and inventive spelling, and mostly appropriate mechanics.	Retelling is lacking one section: beginning, middle, or end. **or** It has less than 3 clues in middle. **or** Retelling is difficult to read with many errors in sentence structure, spelling, and mechanics.	Retelling is lacking two or more sections: beginning, middle, or end. Retelling is difficult to read with many errors in sentence structure, spelling, and mechanics.

Skills Rubric

Task	4	3	2	1
2AS.3 Pronounces words with vowel patterns.	Reads words with ease. 15–16 correct out of 16.	14 correct out of 16.	13–11 correct out of 16.	Fewer than 11 correct out of 16.

Writing Rubric

Task	4	3	2	1
2AW.4 Writes a story which includes a beginning, middle, and end.	Story is creative with several (more than 5) adjectives. It includes well developed beginning, middle, and end. It has a variety of sentence structures, mostly conventional spelling, and appropriate mechanics.	Story is functional and has beginning, middle, and end. It contains a few (3–5) adjectives. Sentence structure is adequate with conventional and inventive spelling, and mostly appropriate mechanics.	Story has all three sections but is written poorly with sentence structure problems, many spelling errors, and inappropriate grammar, capitalization, and punctuation. **or** Story lacks one of the sections of beginning, middle, or end.	Story lacks two or all of the sections and is difficult to understand with numerous errors in sentence structure, spelling, and mechanics.

Oral Reading Record

The Mystery of the Missing Cat Food Part A

Name _____ Date _____

Directions: Ask the child to read the mini-book aloud; record any mistakes here. Put a check (✓) over words read correctly and circle words omitted. If a word is mispronounced or a substitution is made, write the incorrect word over the correct word. If you had to say the word for the student, write T above the word. If an error is repeated over and over again (such as reading *look* for *like* in every sentence), count it as *one error*. If the child says *look* for *like* on one page, reads *like* correctly on the next, and then reads *look* for *like* on another page, count each error. Record your observations about the child's reading behaviors in the comments box.

12 Week Book — *The Mystery of the Missing Cat Food* by Betsy Franco

Text	Comments
It all started the morning that Snowflake's cat food was missing from her bowl.	
"It must be a mouse," my brother Joe said. "But a little mouse just couldn't eat that much food," I said. "It must be something bigger."	
"Let's put out flour all over the kitchen floor. That way we can get some footprints to study," I said.	
When we woke up, we had our prints—lots of them.	
With a book on animal prints from the library, we narrowed it down to a dog.	
Next, we had to figure out how big a dog. "That dog is getting through the cat door so it must be as small as a cat," said Joe.	

Scoring Guide

Orally read with 0–5 errors = 4; 6–11 errors = 3; 12–15 errors = 2; more than 15 errors = 1.

Oral Reading Record

The Mystery of the Missing Cat Food Part B

Name _____ Date _____

Directions: Ask the child to read the mini-book aloud; record any mistakes here. Put a check (✓) over words read correctly and circle words omitted. If a word is mispronounced or a substitution is made, write the incorrect word over the correct word. If you had to say the word for the student, write T above the word. If an error is repeated over and over again (such as reading *look* for *like* in every sentence), count it as *one error*. If the child says *look* for *like* on one page, reads *like* correctly on the next, and then reads *look* for *like* on another page, count each error. Record your observations about the child's reading behaviors in the comments box.

12 Week Book — *The Mystery of the Missing Cat Food* by Betsy Franco

Text	Comments
Joe and I made a list of the dogs in the neighborhood. The only small dogs we knew were Shadow and Rap.	
First we went to see Mrs. Brown, the lady down the street. She owned Shadow. "We never let Shadow out without a leash," she said. "It couldn't be Shadow."	
Next, we went to see Rap's owner. "At night, I just let Rap out for a short run in the dark. He always comes right back," said Mr. Green.	
In came Rap, wagging his tail. "He's been getting a bit chubby lately, hasn't he?" said Mr. Green.	
Joe and I gave each other a thumbs up. We had solved the mystery of the missing cat food!	

Scoring Guide

Orally read with 0–5 errors = 4; 6–11 errors = 3; 12–15 errors = 2; more than 15 errors = 1.

Retelling Form

Name _____ Date _____

Directions: Write the title of the story you read on the first line. Then retell the story in writing.
Remember to include the beginning, middle, and end.

_____

_____

_____

_____

_____

_____

_____

_____

_____

_____

_____

_____

_____

Vowel Patterns Record Sheet

Name _____ Date _____

Directions: Show the child a word card with a nonsense word on it. Say: *I will show you a word card with a nonsense word on it. Say it like it should sound using what you know about letters and the sounds they make.* Record what the student says below. You can ask for the other sound on #13 and #14 so that both the long o and the "ow" as in cow is spoken. For #3 and #15 it can be the long or short e sound.

Note: Students should have practice with nonsense words containing these patterns before the assessment.

1. fleet _____	**9.** preventure _____
2. reblewing _____	**10.** maw _____
3. tweaker _____	**11.** champoo _____
4. smook _____	**12.** tounding _____
5. snoil _____	**13.** slown _____
6. minpention _____	**14.** mowler _____
7. haudit _____	**15.** squeating _____
8. joast _____	**16.** glent _____

Scoring Guide

The student is correct if s/he decodes the words or sounds them out.
0–1 errors = 4; 2 errors = 3; 3–5 errors = 2; more than 5 errors = 1

Grade 2 B Assessment

24 Week Assessment

Note: Individual Student Profile (p. 116) and Class Record Sheet (p. 193) needed for all assessments.

Reading	Assessment Areas	Directions
Grouping: Group **Timeframe:** 20 minutes **Materials:** • *Lost in the Snow* by Betsy Franco; see Appendix • Reading Rubric, p. 125 • Blank paper or stationery	2BR.1 Silently reads text and writes a brief summary.	Distribute copies of the book and read the title together. Say: *This is a story about how two twins, Jack and Jessica, get lost in the snow while skiing and then are rescued. Read to find out how they use their heads in a scary situation.* Ask children to read the book to themselves. Tell them that when they are done they will write a summary of the story. Students can use the book to check the spelling of words and names.
Grouping: Group **Timeframe:** 20–25 minutes **Materials:** • Reading Rubric, p. 125 • Problem-Resolution worksheet, p. 127 • Cloze Exercise, p. 128	2BR.2 Identifies problem of story and ways to solve problem.	Distribute the Problem-Resolution worksheet. Say: *We just read* Lost in the Snow. *Think about the problem the characters faced. Then think about what they did to solve their problem. On this sheet, please write down the problem on the first part, and all the things the characters did to solve their problem on the second part. You can use the book to check the spelling of names and words.*
	2BR.3 Completes a cloze exercise without book use.	Next, distribute the Cloze Exercise for *Lost in the Snow.* Ask students to complete the sentences with words they remember from the story. Students should not use the book for this exercise.
Skills	**Assessment Areas**	**Directions**
Grouping: Group **Timeframe:** 10 minutes **Materials:** • Reading Rubric, p. 125 • Prefixes and Suffixes worksheet, p. 129	2BS.4 Completes sentences using appropriate prefixes and suffixes.	Distribute the Prefixes and Suffixes worksheet. Say: *These sentences all have a word that is missing either a prefix or a suffix. Who can remind us what prefixes are? Suffixes? Good. Let's look at the box on the bottom of the page. I'm going to read these prefixes and suffixes aloud; point to them as I read.* [Read them.] *Okay, now I'd like you to add the right prefix or suffix to each word that is missing a part. Please work on your own.*
Writing	**Assessment Areas**	**Directions**
Grouping: Small group **Timeframe:** 15–20 minutes **Materials:** • Reading Rubric, p. 125 • Blank, lined paper	2BW.5 Writes a story with problem, steps for resolution, and a resolution.	Distribute the writing sheet and say: *Let's talk about* Lost in the Snow. *What was their problem and how did they try to resolve it?* [Discuss.] *Now, I would like you to write a story that has a problem. Include the steps the character(s) follow, and how the problem is actually solved. It can be a real story or make believe.* Lead a discussion of story possibilities and model how you might develop a story. (Examples: Someone lost something. Someone gets lost in the zoo. Child can't decide which pet she wants.) Encourage students to prewrite before beginning their stories.

Reading/Writing Skills Rubric

Task	4	3	2	1
2BR.1 Silently reads text and writes a brief summary.	Writes a complete detailed summary which includes the major events. Events: Jack and Jessica are skiing and lose their dad. They realize they are lost. They do things to save themselves like building a snow cave and putting skis in an X shape outside the cave. The rescue team arrives and they are saved.	Writes a mostly complete summary but some of the events may be somewhat vague. **or** Includes all of the major events but the writing is a detailed retelling and not a summary.	Writes a summary but leaves out one or two events.	Attempts to write a summary but leaves out more than two events.
2BR.2 Identifies problem of story and ways to solve problem.	Identifies problem (Jack and Jessica get lost) and 3 ways they worked to solve problem. Possible Ways to Solve Problem: They yell for help. They build a snow cave. They put their skis in an X shape with red scarf outside cave. They eat food and huddle together.	Identifies problem (Jack and Jessica get lost) and 2 ways they worked to solve problem. Possible Ways to Solve Problem: They yell for help. They build a snow cave. They put their skis in an X shape with red scarf outside cave. They eat food and huddle together.	May or may not identify problem (Jack and Jessica get lost) and 1 way they worked to solve problem. Possible Ways to Solve Problem: They yell for help. They build a snow cave. They put their skis in an X shape with red scarf outside cave. They eat food and huddle together.	Unable to answer question correctly.

Reading/**W**riting **S**kills **R**ubric (Cont.)

Task	4	3	2	I
2BR.3 Completes a cloze exercise without book use.	19–20 correct answers. Correct answers: 1. dad, ski; 2. taken, hear; 3. worried, mountain; 4. cave, time; 5. skis, scarf; 6. cave, found; 7. together, feet; 8. shouting, dogs; 9. crawled, snow; 10. took, you. The correct answers are taken from the text. However, if the student substitutes a word that makes sense in the context of the sentence and story, it is acceptable. For example: for #8, if the student wrote *yelling* instead of *shouting*, it would be acceptable. For #9, if the student wrote *came* instead of *crawled*, it would be acceptable.	17–18 correct answers.	14–16 correct answers.	Fewer than 14 correct answers.
2BS.4 Completes sentences using appropriate prefixes and suffixes.	Completes 5 out of 5 sentences correctly. Answers: 1. non 4. ly 2. re 5. ful 3. ness	Completes 4 out of 5 sentences correctly.	Completes 3 out of 5 sentences correctly.	Completes fewer than 3 out of 5 sentences correctly.
2BW.5 Writes a story with problem, steps for resolution, and a resolution.	Story includes a clear problem and resolution. There are several details (at least 4 details) about the how the problem is solved. The story is appropriately organized and logical. The story has correct sentence structure. There are only a few errors (fewer than 5) in punctuation, capitalization, and spelling.	Story includes a problem and resolution. There are details (at least 3 details) about the how the problem is solved. One of the sections may be somewhat vague. The story is organized but may have a digression. The story has correct sentence structure. There are no more than 10 errors in punctuation, capitalization, and spelling.	Story is missing one aspect (problem, steps for resolution, or resolution). The story lacks organization. The story has errors in punctuation, capitalization, and spelling that make it somewhat difficult to understand.	Story is missing more than one aspect (problem, steps for resolution, or resolution). The story has numerous errors in punctuation, capitalization, and spelling that make it extremely difficult to understand.

Problem-**R**esolution

Name _____ Date _____

Directions: Write the problem of the story *Lost in the Snow* below. Then list as many ways as you can that Jack and Jessica tried to get rescued.

What was the problem in the story?

_____

_____

_____

_____

_____

What did Jack and Jessica do to try and get saved and to be safe?

_____

_____

_____

_____

_____

_____

_____

Cloze Exercise

Name _____ Date _____

Directions: Complete the sentences below from the book *Lost in the Snow*. Think about what happened in the story to help you. You are not allowed to use the book to complete these sentences. Think carefully about how you spell words.

1. Jessica and Jack were way ahead of their _____ on the _____ slope.

2. "We must have _____ a wrong turn off the path," said Jessica. "Hello, hello, does anyone _____ us?" they yelled.

3. The twins became _____ about spending the night on the cold _____ .

4. Together Jack and Jessica dug a snow _____ under a large tree. It took a long _____ .

5. They put their _____ in an X shape and placed Jessica's red _____ around the top of it.

6. Inside the _____, Jack and Jessica searched their pockets. They _____ granola bars they had packed for a snack.

7. Jack and Jessica huddled _____ for over an hour to keep their hands and _____ warm.

8. Then they heard someone _____ ,"Jack! Jessica!" They heard _____ barking, and people talking in an excited way.

9. Jack and Jessica _____ quickly out of the _____ cave.

10. "You _____ a wrong turn. But I can see _____ used your heads."

Prefixes and Suffixes

Name _____ Date _____

Directions: Read the following sentences. One word in each sentence has a part missing. The missing parts are prefixes and suffixes. There is a list of them in the box at the bottom of the page. Write in the prefix or suffix that makes the word make sense in the sentence.

1. What you are talking about is _____sense.

2. The man _____turned to the store to get his present.

3. Mark shows much kind_____ to other people.

4. The girl walked slow_____ to the door because she was afraid.

5. Sue was joy_____ when she got her new puppy.

> **Prefix and Suffix Bank**
>
> re-   non-   -ly   -ful   -ness

Grade 2 C Assessment

36 Week Assessment

Note: Individual Student Profile (p. 116) and Class Record Sheet (p.193) needed for all assessments.

Reading	Assessment Areas	Directions
Grouping: Group **Timeframe:** 20–30 minutes **Materials:** • *Jane Goodall and the Chimps*, see Appendix • Reading Guide, p. 132	2CR.I Silently reads text and responds to questions.	Distribute books to the class and say, *Today you will be reading a book about Jane Goodall and her work with animals, especially chimpanzees. Jane studied the chimps in Africa. She wrote and spoke about her work with the chimps so that people would understand how important it is to take care of wild animals and their habitats or where they live.* *First, look at your reading guide. You will be answering the questions after you read the book. I will read the questions as you follow along.* Read the questions aloud; then tell students they can begin reading. The students need to read and then answer the questions. Students can use the book as they answer the questions.
Writing	**Assessment Areas**	**Directions**
Grouping: Group **Timeframe:** 20 minutes **Materials:** • Reading/Writing Rubric, p. 131 • Blank, lined paper	2CW.2 Writes a response to a question with appropriate supporting details from the text.	Say: *Jane Goodall cared about animals. Write a short piece about how you know she cared about animals using the story you just read. Include at least two ways the story shows you that she cared about animals. Be sure to write carefully using appropriate spelling, capitalization, and punctuation.* Write the prompt on the board or on chart paper, and encourage students to prewrite.

Reading/Writing Rubric

Task	4	3	2	1
2CR.1 Silently reads text and responds to questions.	Correctly completes reading guide (4 points). Responses are well written with appropriate mechanics. Reading Guide answers: 1. see p. 3 for correctness (1 pt.) 2. see pp. 4–9 for correctness (1 pt.) 3. any two facts in story (2 pts.)	Completes Reading Guide but may have one response that is neither completely correct nor incorrect (3 pts. out of 4 pts.). Responses are understandable with mostly appropriate mechanics.	Reading Guide responses are 2 pts. out of 4 correct. Writing is somewhat difficult to read.	Reading Guide score is less than 2 pts. Responses are difficult to read.
2CW.2 Writes a response to a question with appropriate supporting details from the text.	Well-written response with appropriate mechanics that describes Jane's love of animals with two supporting details included. Possible details: –when young watched animals and birds near home –when four years old, watched hen house –goes to Africa to be with wild animals –studies chimps –gives names to chimps –shared nuts with chimps –wrote books on chimps –speaks to people about chimps	Complete response but one detail may be vague. Writing is mostly well written with appropriate mechanics.	Response is readable but lacking in one of the details.	Response is difficult to read and has vague details or no details.

Reading Guide

for Jane Goodall and the Chimps

Name _____ Date _____

Directions: Look over the questions below. Answer them after you read the book. You can use your book to reread and find the answers to the questions. You may use another sheet of paper if you need more space.

1. Why did Jane go to Africa?

_____

_____

_____

_____

_____

_____

2. Name one thing Jane did while she was in Africa.

_____

_____

_____

_____

_____

_____

3. List two facts about *Jane Goodall and the Chimps.*

_____

_____

_____

_____

Chapter 10

Introduction to the Interventions

The assessments in Chapters 7–9 identify areas in which students need further instruction. The next four chapters help you select activities that reteach and reinforce essential literacy skills in each of the four categories: print conventions, word recognition development, comprehension, and writing.

But first, let's examine a teaching model that has proven effective for administering the interventions. This six-part framework helps you individualize instruction and identify when a particular method is not working for a student.

1. Break down the task into parts.
2. Demonstrate the task or part for the learner.
3. Support the learner while s/he tries the task or part.
4. Provide feedback to the learner about his/her work.
5. Repeat items 2–4 until you're giving minimal support.
6. Learner independently tries task or part. If performance does not meet expectations, repeat steps 1–5, using another method, if possible.

Let's look at an example of how this model might look in action. Mrs. Cooper is teaching her second graders how to write summaries of stories. One student, Tom, is having trouble with this task. He has a tendency to leave out a key section of the story when he writes a summary, and he uses too much detail. Tom needs instruction about including the beginning, middle, and end in a summary, and about separating main idea and details.

Using the model described above to address Tom's problem, Mrs. Cooper would proceed as follows.

1. Break down the task into parts. Tom's problem can be broken down into two main parts. He has difficulty with identifying the beginning, middle, and end of stories. He also has difficulty with generalizing ideas or selecting the main events of the story. For each of these two difficulties, Mrs. Cooper plans intervention instruction. First, she decides to help Tom develop an understanding of beginning, middle, and end. She breaks this task down into three parts: highlighting beginning, middle, and end in short stories; identifying when a beginning, middle, or end is missing; and writing complete summaries. Mrs. Cooper will tackle the second part of the problem, selecting main events, through a similar process once Tom has mastered the first part.

2–6. Highlight beginning, middle, and end. Mrs. Cooper gives Tom large index cards with simple stories written on them. She asks Tom to highlight the beginning, middle, and end of each story after demonstrating how to do the first one. She provides feedback support as Tom practices, gradually reducing the amount of feedback until Tom can highlight the beginning, middle, and end of a story independently.

2–6. Identify missing components of a summary. Now that Tom is confident about identifying the beginning, middle, and end of stories, Mrs. Cooper gives him some stories with one of those pieces missing. She models how she figures out which part is missing, and then asks Tom to do the same for a different story. Again, she provides support and feedback until Tom can complete the task independently.

2–6. Write complete summaries. Now that Tom can identify the parts and recognize when something is missing, Mrs. Cooper reads him a folk tale (folk tales are usually short and always include a definitive beginning, middle, and end) and models writing a complete summary. After thinking aloud through the first summary, Mrs. Cooper reads another folk tale and has Tom write the summary, with her support. Over the next few days, she asks Tom to read and summarize a few more short texts, until he can do so confidently.

Once Tom has mastered identifying the beginning, middle, and end of a story, Mrs. Cooper moves on to his second difficulty, providing too many details in a summary, and repeats the instructional process.

1. Break the task into parts. She breaks this task into two parts: identifying "just-right" summaries and then writing just-right summaries.

2–6. Identify Just-Right Summaries. Mrs. Cooper prepares sets of summaries for several short stories. For the first story, she writes three summaries—one has too much detail, one not enough, and one is just right. (All the summaries contain a beginning, middle, and end, so Tom can focus on the issue of including appropriate details.) She reads the story with Tom, and then she reads the summaries, thinking aloud for him about the amount of detail each contains. Once Tom seems to grasp what a just-right summary is, Mrs. Cooper has him work through a story and decide if the accompanying summary is too detailed, too sparse, or just right. Then she has him practice with a few more stories until he can identify a just-right summary confidently and consistently.

2–6. Write Just-Right Summaries. Now Mrs. Cooper wants Tom to translate his knowledge of just-right summaries to his own summary writing. She reads aloud a folk tale and then composes a summary for Tom. The next day, she reads another story and works with Tom to write the summary, providing support and feedback. Then she has Tom write summaries independently, giving support as needed, until he can consistently write a just-right summary.

Following a step-by-step instructional sequence supports individual learners where they need it most. As you're planning intervention instruction, keep this model in mind.

In the next few chapters several intervention activities, techniques, and strategies are provided for the four aspects of literacy for the primary grades: print conventions, word recognition/oral fluency/word study, comprehension, and writing. These interventions are various ways to accomplish the complex task of teaching students to read and write in grades K–2. There are also many more ideas that you already have or that other educators use. Our collaboration and sharing of ideas will help us be successful at this significant task, and implementing those ideas within the six-part framework outlined in this chapter will increase the possibilities of success.

Chapter 11

Intervention Instruction for Print Conventions

Print conventions include book familiarity (location of print, where to start reading, and what direction to read and write), text features (punctuation, capitalization, and special types like boldface), and text concepts (word boundaries, number of words/letters, and first/last part of word/sentence). Teaching print conventions gives children the tools they need to delve into a text and begin reading. As Clay (1993a) points out, this group of behaviors supports the acquisition of literacy. While these conventions are second nature for us as experienced readers, it's important to remember how foreign they seem to new readers. Students need direct instruction about them and plenty of practice with them so that using them becomes routine. It is important that these print conventions are not taken too lightly because they can become stumbling blocks in the future if not learned in the early years.

Factors That Influence the Learning of Print Conventions

There are several factors that influence how easily students can grasp print conventions. These include:

◉ auditory memory for words,

◉ visual memory for features (period, colon, capitals, boldface type),

◉ understanding of purpose or concepts for these features, and

◉ frequency of experience with these features in different types of text.

In looking at these factors that can influence the learning of print conventions, it is clear that memory plays a significant role. Auditory memory, or things remembered from listening, and visual memory, or things remembered from observing, are critical perceptual aspects of all literacy learning. The intervention activities for memory are provided in this chapter but are applicable to word recognition, comprehension, and writing as well.

Recommended Best Practices for Learning Print Conventions

First of all, teachers should demonstrate daily how print conventions are useful in both reading and writing. As Clay (1991, 1993a, 1993b) points out, print conventions are best learned in the context of reading authentic text, which happens throughout the day. Opportunities occur during guided reading, where a discussion of print conventions can naturally emerge during the preview, reading, or follow-up stages of a lesson. In addition, I've found that composing stories on chart paper with guided reading groups is an excellent way to model and reinforce the print conventions we notice during our reading. Using Big Books during shared reading and read aloud also facilitates discussion of print conventions; since the text is visible to all, it's easy to pause and quickly discuss a punctuation mark or other text convention without disrupting the flow of the reading. Shared writing is the perfect time to model the use of print conventions, which students can then put into practice during their independent writing time.

Moreover, teachers should provide students with multiple experiences with various print conventions through a variety of types of texts in the reading and writing material they use in instruction. Children will require much practice in the identification, understanding, and use of these print conventions.

Intervention Activities for Print Conventions

The rest of this chapter provides intervention activities to help students develop their understanding of print conventions. The chart on the next pages links the intervention activities with the assessment benchmarks for easy reference. For instance, if a first grader is having difficulty isolating words in print (1AR.4), the chart points you to the appropriate intervention activity; in this case, Text Concepts.

One caveat: As I noted earlier in this chapter, auditory and visual memory can often hamper a child's ability to learn print conventions. You will need to determine if the print convention hasn't been learned because of lack of skill, knowledge, or memory. For example, if the child has difficulty remembering names for things or visually identifying the differences between words, then it might be useful to include memory activities along with the specific assessment item activity.

Chart of Print Conventions
Expectations/Assessment Items/Intervention Activities

Kindergarten Expectations	Assessment Items	Intervention Activities
• Identify where the print is on the page.	KAR.1 Finds front of book; finds back of book.	Print Conventions: Book Familiarity
• Identify the cover of the book.	KAR.2 Understands print is on page.	Print Conventions: Book Familiarity
• Identify the title of the book.	KAR.3 Follows story read.	Print Conventions: Text Concepts
• Understand which way to read (left to right).	KAR.4 Knows reading goes from left to right.	Print Conventions: Book Familiarity
	KBR.1 Points to title.	Print Conventions: Book Familiarity
• Identify the word boundaries of the print.	KBR.2 Understands directionality/voice-print match.	Print Conventions: Book Familiarity/Text Concepts
• Demonstrate voice-print match.	KBR.4 Identifies period with purpose.	Print Conventions: Text Features
• Identify and understand purpose of period and question mark.	KBR.5 Counts words in sentence.	Print Conventions: Text Concepts
	KBR.6 Counts letters in word.	Print Conventions: Text Concepts
	KCR.1 Points to title.	Print Conventions: Book Familiarity
	KCR.2 Understands directionality/voice-print match.	Print Conventions: Book Familiarity/Text Concepts
	KCR.4 Identifies question mark with purpose.	Print Conventions: Text Features
	KCR.5 Counts words in sentence.	Print Conventions: Text Concepts
	KCR.6 Counts letters in word.	Print Conventions: Text Concepts

Grade 1 Expectations	Assessment Items	Intervention Activities
• Understand how the text moves from line to line, or return sweep.	1AR.1 Points to the title.	Print Conventions: Book Familiarity
	1AR.3 Points to three words when given by teacher.	Print Conventions: Text Concepts
• Understand the meaning of boldface, italic, and all-caps type.	1AR.4 Isolates one and two letters and words in print.	Print Conventions: Text Concepts
• Identify and understand punctuation: exclamation point, comma, quotation marks, in addition to periods and question marks.	1AR.6 Identifies and explains use of question mark and exclamation point.	Print Conventions: Text Features
	1BR.3 Identifies and explains the use of comma and quotation marks.	Print Conventions: Text Features
• Demonstrate voice-print match consistently.		

Grade 2 Expectations	Assessment Items	Intervention Activities
• Understand different text formats and graphics. • Use and interpret graphs, graphic organizers, picture captions, indexes, table of contents, and glossaries.	No specific assessment items in grade 2 assessments.	Teacher can use the activities from first grade that correspond to any difficulties second graders may have with print conventions.

☑ Memory Activities

Memory plays a significant role in all learning. The following memory activities can help improve both the auditory and visual memories. These activities are included in the Print Conventions section because students will need memory abilities beginning with these understandings and continuing through Word Recognition, Comprehension, and Writing.

AUDITORY MEMORY

Auditory memory involves remembering things heard. Children need to be able to remember abstract names for figures, such as *question mark* for *?*, in addition to terms such as *letters*, *words*, and *sentences*. The Unrelated Words activities attempt to strengthen the ability to remember abstractions. The Related Words activities involve memorizing sentences that have a context or meaning, to aid in remembering.

Unrelated Words

Name the Object: Level 1. Select seven objects for use in this game (such as a spoon, fork, pencil, eraser, ball, bracelet, and dinosaur). Say the name of each object as you show them to students. If a student doesn't readily identify an object being used, select another that is more easily recognizable. Read off combinations of three items at a time. Then ask students to pick out the objects you just named in the order you said them. Students receive one point for each correct pattern of objects completed. The student with the most points wins. As students become more proficient with the game, increase the number of objects you read, working up to seven.

Name the Object: Level 2. Play the same game as in level 1, using objects and a few of the students' known word cards. Intersperse the words with the objects when asking them to recall patterns. If playing the game in a group, be sure all students in the group know the word card.

Name the Object: Level 3. Play the same game as in level 1 but use known word cards only. Again, all students in the group will need to know the word cards.

Related Words or Sentences

Memory Sentences. Read a sentence and have students repeat it. They need to repeat the words exactly in order to be correct. Sentences should begin with 5 words and increase over time to 12 words.

Words	Sample Sentences:
5	I had a party today.
	Saturday is my tenth birthday.
6	I like pears and sometimes plums.
	The teacher is kind and good.
7	Trees are brown and green in color.
	We buy food in the grocery store.
8	Tomorrow is a big day in my life.
	Thursday is game day for all the students.
9	Valentine's Day is a very fun day for me.
	Bowling is a fun sport that everyone should play.
10	Tomorrow we will begin our long trip to Sandy Beach.
	We take our vacation in July when it is hot.
11	I would like to paint my room blue with white trim.
	Can we have chocolate cake with peach and banana ice cream?
12	Yesterday, we went to the zoo and saw the big gray elephants.
	Let's carefully plan our vacation to England for the month of July.

VISUAL MEMORY

Ten-Second Memory Game. Present objects to the students and have them look at them for about ten seconds. Then hide the objects and ask students to recall what they saw. Begin with a small number of objects (3 to 5) and increase to 10 to 12 objects.

Concentration. This familiar game, in which players turn over cards and try to match pairs, is an excellent visual memory activity. The cards can have letters, words, or pictures on them, depending on the level of the students. Students take turns and turn over two cards to see if they match. If they match, the student gets the cards and an extra turn. If there is no match, the player's turn ends. The next player takes a turn. When all the cards have been collected, the player with the most cards wins. Cards for this concentration game can be made up and should relate to what is presently being taught in any subject area. For the visual memory practice, students **do not** read the letters or words, or say the picture. They are just using visual cues.

Look, Remember, Draw. For this fun activity, hold up a simple design for students to look at for about ten seconds. Then challenge students to replicate the design on a sheet of paper. The designs should become more complicated.

☑ Book Familiarity Activities

Find the Feature. In addition to modeling book handling during guided and shared reading and read aloud, you can give students hands-on practice finding book features with this fun activity. Select several books and place them randomly on a table (for example, some will be upside down, others will be face down, etc.). First, ask students to rearrange the books so that the covers are face up. Next, have students point to all the titles. Then mix up the books again and have students put them so only the backs are showing. This activity can be done as a game if each child is given a set of books. A point is scored if the books are all correct, or you can give one point for each correct book, depending on the child's skill. Or students can work together in small groups to complete the tasks.

Follow the Print. Listening to taped books and following along by pointing to the printed text is excellent practice for developing directionality in reading, especially the return sweep. Start children with simple books and work up to more print. Model how to point to text until students feel confident pointing on their own. A more advanced activity, Follow the Words, is on page 116.

☑ Text Features Activities

On Your Mark. Help students recognize punctuation and read it effectively with this easy activity. Give each student a set of index cards with one punctuation mark written on each. Before you read a book (Big Books work well), tell students what to look for; as you read, when they see the mark, they hold up their matching index card. Ask them what they notice about how the mark is used and how your voice changed when you read the words around the mark. The cards can be used for many other activities, such as the following one.

Punctuate That Sentence! Select several sentences to read aloud, and write them on a chart without using punctuation. Give students sticky notes with one punctuation mark written on each. Then read the sentence and ask students to put the sticky notes with the appropriate punctuation marks where they need to be. As students place marks, discuss the purpose of each.

Punctuating Poetry. Reading poetry aloud is a great way for students to practice reading punctuation appropriately. Each time they come to a punctuation mark, have them make that mark in the air. This heightened awareness of punctuation marks will help them read with expression and use punctuation in their own writing. This activity can also be done with regular text, but poetry has a higher frequency of different types of punctuation compared to some primary texts, and is an appealing genre for children.

☑ Text Concepts Activities

Follow the Words. Similar to Follow the Print on page 141, in this activity children listen to taped stories and follow along in the book. This time, they match each word they hear to one on the page, developing voice-print match and one-to-one correspondence. They will need to turn the pages as they listen.

Focus on Words. For practice with word boundaries and understanding the number of words on a page or letters in word, have students use index cards or two fingers to isolate words and letters in lines of print.

Cut It Up. To develop students' understanding of words and letters, write a sentence on a sentence strip or chart paper. Ask students to cut up the sentence into words. They can then count the number of words and reassemble the sentence. For a more advanced version, after students have reassembled the words into a sentence, have them cut up the words into letters. They then count the number of letters in each word and reassemble the words.

Pointing Fingers. Having students use their fingers to point to the text as it is read to them or with them helps them develop an awareness of voice-print match, the understanding that each group of letters makes up a word that corresponds to a spoken word. You can use a stick or pointer to model this kind of reading with Big Books. Word pointing should be done as students read until they understand the concept. However, if children point continuously to their reading, it may cause them to be choppy readers. Encouraging them to practice without finger-pointing and to stop using fingers once they grasp one-to-one correspondence can alleviate this problem. Certainly by the end of grade 2, all students should be reading without the aid of a finger. Using a bookmark under the line of text to be read can be helpful in transitioning students from pointing to non-pointing.

Sentence Walk. This fun, interactive activity helps students understand voice-print match and word boundaries. Write a sentence using large letters on sentence strips or chart paper. Cut the words apart and place them on the floor, in order and spaced a child's step apart. Slowly read the sentences aloud and have students step on each word as it is read. This activity works nicely with nursery rhymes because they are short and rhythmic.

Counting Words. During guided reading, have children find one sentence and count the number of words in it. Also, have students look at a word and tell you the number of letters in the word.

Read-a-Word. Using a familiar book, have students read the first word of the sentence and then the last word of the sentence. Or have them read the third word, fifth word, and so on. This quick practice will help children develop the concepts of sentence and word. For letters, use one word and ask them to say the first letter, the last letter, and so on.

☑ Parent Home Activities for Print Conventions

Many of the following activities are done with a read aloud book; you will want to use age-appropriate books on your child's reading level. Be sure to follow suggestions from the classroom teacher.

MEMORY ACTIVITIES

Visual Memory. Place four or five household objects on a tray or cookie sheet and cover them with a towel. Explain to your child that you are going to display the objects for 15 seconds. Then you will cover them and ask your child to name as many of the items as possible. If your child can name all five, then increase the number by two or three. Play several times.

Auditory Memory. While your child is doing everyday things, such as getting ready for school, ask him or her to follow three simple directions. For example, you might say, "first, put your shirt on, then put your jeans on, and lastly, put your sneakers on." If your child can easily perform the directions in this way, increase the number slowly. Change the directions around each time you play the game to see if he or she can remember them in a different order.

TEXT FEATURES AND CONCEPTS

Read Aloud. Select an appropriate book to read to your child. As you read the book aloud, point out the text features that he/she is learning in school. For example, if your child is studying quotation marks, ask him/her to find the quotation marks in the book as you read. Your child can also repeat what you read in quotes to help draw his/her attention to the quotation marks.

Follow Along. After you have read aloud a book, reread it and ask your child to point to the words with you and follow along. Let your child join in with the reading where she/he remembers the parts. A book that is repetitive works well for this activity.

Questioning. After reading a book aloud, question your child about the text features being studied in school, such as periods, question marks, words, and sentences. As you complete a page, ask your child questions such as "How many words are there on this page?" "How many question marks do you see?"

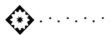

Chapter 12

Intervention Instruction for Word Recognition Development

In grades K–2, word recognition, which includes cueing strategies, oral fluency, and word study, is the predominant area of instruction for students. It is important to get students recognizing words and reading fluently in the primary grades so they can focus on the more complex comprehension skills and strategies in the intermediate grades. Getting children to read automatically frees the memory load of the brain and allows concentration on higher-level comprehension (Perfetti, 1985). If students require a great deal of processing time in order to read unfamiliar words, their ability to comprehend will be diminished. However, this task is complex and requires a few years of appropriate instruction.

The three strands of word recognition—cueing strategies, oral fluency, and word study—will be discussed separately in this chapter. However, in instruction they need to be emphasized simultaneously unless a specific weakness has been identified. These activities can be used for initial instruction as well as for reteaching. I suggest that oral reading records be taken frequently during these instructional years, not just at the assessment dates. The errors and the positive behaviors identified in these oral reading records are windows into how the student is acquiring word recognition ability (Pearson & Stephens, 1994).

Since all three of the areas (cueing strategies, oral fluency, and word study) need to be taught together, I will begin by discussing effective instruction for word recognition in the guided reading setting. As a result of this instruction or from your assessments, you may identify an area of need for your students. You will find specific intervention activities for these areas in the last section.

Recommended Best Practices for Word Recognition

In order to understand what needs adjustment in word recognition instruction, let's first look at what effective instruction looks like in guided reading groups. The following are elements of effective instruction:

1. Identify reading levels/needs.
2. Select the appropriate level book for students' competencies.
3. Design a lesson to address needs.
4. Use appropriate intervention strategies during the lesson in response to students.
5. Assess learning and the lesson to determine next steps.

1. IDENTIFY READING LEVELS/NEEDS

Initially, you need to know the reading level of each of your students. The diagnostic placement assessments for each grade level will help you determine your students' strengths and needs, and identify their reading levels.

2. SELECT THE APPROPRIATE LEVEL BOOK FOR STUDENTS' COMPETENCIES

Once you've identified a student's reading level and needs, choose a book that provides the appropriate support and challenge to move him or her ahead. In order for students to pass through the various phases of word recognition, they need to be reading books that support their use of cueing strategies. There are several leveling systems that rank books by degree of challenge to help you with the selection process (Weaver, 2000; Fountas & Pinnell, 1996; Schulman & Payne, 2000). The Reading Recovery® system is a specific tutorial program, which can be difficult to use in general classroom instruction, especially because it is primarily a grade 1 system. However, the books are leveled to provide a progression of challenge. It is important to use one of the leveling systems so that you can provide this progression of competencies. Some teachers develop their own system, but using an established system and then modifying it for your needs is a more practical solution since it is difficult to create a system.

If students use a text that is leveled too high for them, they will stumble over words and become frustrated. An appropriate book provides students with some unfamiliar words, but not too many. In other words, students should be reading at their instructional level of reading during guided reading or be at a level in which they can read 95 percent of the words with accuracy and comprehend 75 percent of the text (Harris & Hodges, 1995). Some suggested levels for guided reading text as a result of giving the assessments in this book are listed below. Also, keep in mind that students who score below the standard on a kindergarten oral reading record probably need more instruction in **literacy readiness**, which includes language experience stories, book handling skills, and listening to stories.

Levels of Books for Instruction*

(*These are approximate levels. There is not a direct relationship or comparison between the various leveling systems. Some books are leveled by the system outside the range listed.)

Instructional Book Levels As a Result of Kindergarten Assessments

Assessments Results	Weaver Literacy Levels	Guided Reading Levels*	Schulman and Payne Levels	Reading Recovery Levels	Traditional Basal Levels
KAR.3 Score of 1 or 2	Emergent A (EmA)	A	Emergent	1	Readiness
KAR.3 Score of 3 or 4	Emergent B (EmB)	B	Emergent	2	Readiness
KBR.3 Score of 1 or 2	Emergent A (EmA)	A	Emergent	1	Readiness
KBR.3 Score of 3 or 4	Emergent B (EmB)	B–C	Emergent	2–3	Readiness
KCR.3 Score of 1 or 2	Emergent B (EmB)	B–C	Emergent	2–3	Readiness
KCR.3 Score of 3 or 4	Early 1 A (E1A) - Early 1 B (E1B)	C–D	Progressing	4–7	Preprimer

Instructional Book Levels As a Result of Grade 1 Assessments

Assessments Results	Weaver Literacy Levels	Guided Reading Levels*	Schulman and Payne Levels	Reading Recovery Levels	Traditional Basal Levels
1AR.2 Score of 1 or 2	Early 1 A (E1A) - Early 1 B (E1B)	C–D	Progressing	4–7	Preprimer 1
1AR.2 Score of 3 or 4	Early 2 A (E2A) - Early 2 B (E2B)	E–F	Progressing	8–10	Preprimer 2
1BR.1 Score of 1 or 2	Early 2 A (E2A) - Early 2 B (E2B)	E–F	Progressing	8–10	Preprimer 2
1BR.1 Score of 3 or 4	Early 3 (E3)	G–H	Transitional	11–13	Preprimer 3
1CR.1 Score of 1 or 2	Early 3 (E3)	G–H	Transitional	11–13	Preprimer 3
1CR.1 Score of 3 or 4	Early 4 (E4)	I	Transitional	14–16	Grade 1

Note: These are approximate levels due to the variety of leveling systems and the inability to have direct relationships between the leveling systems.

* Guided Reading Levels as described by Fountas and Pinnell in *Guided Reading* (1996).

Instructional Book Levels As a Result of Grade 2 Assessments

Assessments Results	Weaver Literacy Levels	Guided Reading Levels*	Schulman and Payne Levels	Reading Recovery Levels	Traditional Basal Levels
2AR.1 Score of 1 or 2	Early 4 (E4)	I	Transitional	14–16	Grade 1
2AR.1 Score of 3 or 4	Fluency 1 (F1)	J–K	Fluent	17–18	Grade 2
2BR.1 Score of 1 or 2	Fluency 1 (F1)	J–K	Fluent	17–18	Grade 2
2BR.1 Score of 3 or 4	Fluency 2 (F2)	L–M	Fluent	20–22	Grade 2
2CR.1 Score of 1 or 2	Fluency 2 (F2)	L–M	Fluent	20–22	Grade 2
2CR.1 Score of 3 or 4	Fluency 3 (F3)	N–O	Fluent	23–24	Grade 3

Note: These are approximate levels due to the variety of leveling systems and the inability to have direct relationships between the leveling systems.

* Guided Reading Levels as described by Fountas and Pinnell in *Guided Reading* (1996).

3. DESIGN A LESSON TO ADDRESS NEEDS

Once you've identified the appropriate level of book and current needs of a student or group of students, it's time to create a balanced lesson plan. In this section, I focus on the components of the word recognition part of the lesson plan, although I recommend that each lesson incorporate skills in all four literacy areas: print conventions, word recognition, comprehension, and writing.

In the area of word recognition, lessons need to focus on direct instruction of cueing strategies, word study, and vocabulary development. The direct instruction should be short and build on previous learning. For example, when working on the visual or grapho-phonics cueing strategy, a teacher might instruct students in the *ame* pattern or have them do a practice sheet on identifying the initial sounds of pictured objects. In addition to direct instruction, incorporating oral reading of familiar books increases oral fluency and is excellent practice for developing word recognition skills. Lesson duration should be about 15 minutes.

A good rule of thumb is to plan two or three lessons with a word recognition focus per week. The initial reading of the text is one lesson (where students practice cueing strategies and oral fluency); then you provide direct instruction for the other two lessons (vocabulary development and phonics instruction). I recommend using one book per week for instruction in guided reading. Not all books will lend themselves to five lessons, but rereading a text ensures that the students have enough practice with the book to become fluent and learn the vocabulary.

4. USE APPROPRIATE INTERVENTION STRATEGIES DURING THE LESSON IN RESPONSE TO STUDENTS

Students will have a difficult time increasing their skills in word recognition unless they are corrected while they are reading. Learning to intervene appropriately and effectively is an important teacher skill that requires staff development and experience. *Guided Reading: Making It Work* by Mary Browning Schulman and Carleen daCruz Payne (Scholastic, 2000) is an excellent resource that describes this skill clearly. The text is easy to understand, provides all the appropriate prompts charted for easy accessibility, and contains numerous ideas about how to use the prompts in the guided reading setting.

Schulman and Payne focus on the three cueing strategies of meaning, structure, and visual/grapho-phonics. A teacher needs to be able to quickly identify which strategy the student is using and not using as he or she reads. Then the teacher must lead a discussion with the child to encourage the use of an appropriate strategy. This technique is critical for teachers to learn so they can help their students use cueing strategies effectively.

Here are some examples of what errors look like, the strategies that are and are not being used, and the appropriate discussion questions for the student. Errors should be discussed right after the student has finished reading the sentence in which the error occurs. In this way, the student will be less likely to lose comprehension of what he or she is reading. This direct instruction intervention is critical to the reader so that he or she can develop the strategies.

Appropriate Interventions During Reading

Note: The Sentence column shows what the student read; the actual text is shown in brackets after the error.

Sentence	Cueing Strategies	Discussion with Child
The dog is racing [running] home.	Used: meaning, structure Not used effectively: visual We know this because the child made the sentence make sense (using meaning cue) and the words were so similar that the child failed to look carefully (use visual cues) while reading.	Teacher says to the child: "Look at the word you called *racing*. Put your finger under it and say it slowly. Do the letters say the sounds in *racing*? What small word do you see in it?" Teacher points to *run*. Student pronounces word and/or teacher says it. Student rereads sentence and then continues reading.

Sentence	Cueing Strategies	Discussion with Child
The mouse is winning [white].	Used: structure, some visual (initial letter) Not used effectively: meaning The student used the structure of the sentence appropriately by saying *winning* but meaning was not very effective because it didn't match the story picture (picture of white mouse). Child was almost making up his/her own story while reading. The child used the *w* in the word to say another word that begins with *w* but needed to look further into the word.	Teacher says: "It doesn't make sense to me. Let's look at the pictures and see if *winning* makes sense. What might make better sense?" Teacher guides the child to understand the word is *white*. Student rereads sentence and then continues reading.
Many [Mary] is a nice girl.	Used: visual Not used: structure, meaning This student was not thinking about what s/he was reading because *many* is not a girl. Also, *many* is an adjective and in this case is being used as a noun (failure to use appropriate language structure). However, the visual aspects of the word are identical with the exception of one letter.	Teacher says to child: "*Many* doesn't sound right to me. Can *many* be a girl? *Many* usually talks about things such as many toys or many animals. What might make better sense here?" Teacher assists child if s/he is unable to pronounce the name *Mary*. Student rereads sentence and then continues reading.
Tommy, will you comb [come] here?	Used: visual (final e rule) Not used: meaning, structure In this case, the student is focusing on phonics rules or patterns (*ome*), or visual cues. *Comb* does not make sense (meaning) and does not fit the language structure of the sentence (structure).	Teacher says to child: "What you read doesn't make sense to me. Reread the sentence again to me." Often this rereading will correct the error. If not, then point to the word and say it. Student rereads sentence and then continues reading.

The goal is for children to apply and integrate all three strategies effectively, always keeping the meaning strategy as the priority. All error words should be taught to the child in the vocabulary development lesson unless they are names of people or things that are unusual.

5. ASSESS LEARNING AND THE LESSON TO DETERMINE NEXT STEPS

Your informal assessments of students during guided reading, along with regular oral reading records and discussions with individuals, will guide your planning of the next lesson. The assessments in this text will give you a complete view of a child's progress periodically through the year, to augment your regular classroom assessments and help you focus instruction.

 ## Intervention Activities for Word Recognition

The following chart summarizes the expectations (described fully in Chapter 3), assessment items, and intervention activities for word recognition.

Chart of Word Recognition
Expectations/Assessment Items/Intervention Activities

Kindergarten Expectations	Assessment Items	Intervention Activities
• Understand that pictures help tell the story.	KBR.3 Reads fluently.	Word Recognition Development: Cueing Strategies
• Understand that the language is segmented into words, and words are segmented into parts or syllables.	KBS.8 Segments words in sentences.	Word Recognition Development: Segmentation
	KBS.9 Segments syllables in words.	Word Recognition Development: Segmentation
	KCR.3 Reads fluently.	Word Recognition Development: Cueing Strategies
	KCS.8 Segments words in sentences.	Word Recognition Development: Segmentation
	KCS.9 Segments syllables in words.	Word Recognition Development: Segmentation

Grade 1 Expectations	Assessment Items	Intervention Activities
• Develop meaning, structure, and visual or grapho-phonic (sound/symbol) cueing strategies.	1AR.2 Orally reads text using strategies.	Word Recognition Development: Cueing Strategies
	1AR.7 Identifies words from similar words when said by teacher.	Word Recognition Development: Visual Cueing Strategy
• Begin to apply all three cueing systems and learn sight vocabulary.	1AS.8 Identifies initial consonants in words.	Word Recognition Development: Phonics
• Attend more to text than to pictures.	1AS.9 Identifies final consonants in words.	Word Recognition Development: Phonics
• Apply knowledge of initial and final sounds along with short, long, and r-controlled vowels.	1BR.1 Orally reads text using strategies.	Word Recognition Development: Cueing Strategies
	1BR.5 Reads familiar sight vocabulary words.	Word Recognition Development: Word Study
• Segment words into sounds and distinguish sounds in words.	1BS.6 Identifies initial blends and digraphs in words.	Word Recognition Development: Phonics
• Self-correct errors when reading.	1BS.7 Segments sounds in words.	Word Recognition Development: Segmentation
• Begin to read text with fluency, including expression.	1CR.1 Orally reads text using strategies.	Word Recognition Development: Cueing Strategies
	1CS.4 Pronounces words with vowel patterns.	Word Recognition Development: Phonics
	1CS.5 Identifies words from which contractions are made.	Word Recognition Development: Word Study
	1CS.6 Identifies appropriate word ending for sentences.	Word Recognition Development: Word Study

Grade 2 Expectations	Assessment Items	Intervention Activities
• Achieve oral fluency. • Read much of their texts silently. • Integrate and apply meaning, structure, and visual (graphophonic) cueing strategies. • Readily learn vocabulary from reading. • Understand the meaning of affixes and how they can change the meaning of root or base words.	2AR.1 Orally reads text using strategies. 2AS.3 Pronounces words with vowel patterns. 2BS.4 Completes sentences using appropriate prefixes and suffixes.	Word Recognition Development: Cueing Strategies Word Recognition Development: Phonics Word Recognition Development: Word Study

☑ Literacy Readiness

During the first semester of kindergarten, teachers focus instruction on very early literacy activities such as language experience stories, oral language development games, picture drawing, alphabet games, writing letters and words, book handling skills, and listening skills. These literacy readiness activities are an important prerequisite to instruction in cueing strategies, oral fluency, and word study. If your students are in first grade and struggling with word recognition skills, be sure to evaluate their literacy readiness and consider including more early literacy activities in your curriculum. A good indicator that students need more early literacy experiences is a score in the 1 to 2 range on every item of the Grade 1A Assessment. Second-language learners often need extensive work in literacy readiness before they can progress.

☑ Cueing Strategies

As stated before in this chapter, it is difficult to separate the cueing strategies from oral fluency or from word study. However, here are some specific techniques and activities that might be helpful to you. Keep in mind that the best technique or method for teaching cueing strategies is modeling during oral reading and providing lots of reading practice.

Factors That Influence Students' Use of Cueing Strategies

◆ amount of oral reading practice with direct instruction of the strategies while reading

- ◆ types of books which permit practice in the cueing strategies
- ◆ ability to integrate strategies and use appropriately
- ◆ degree of skill with each strategy
- ◆ English language ability

CUEING STRATEGY: MEANING

The goal of all reading is to make meaning from text. From the very beginning we need to make students aware that what they're reading should make sense. Helping them self-monitor for meaning and use meaning as a cueing strategy—i.e., asking, What would make sense here?—is crucial for beginning readers.

Since the meaning cue is dependent on one's knowledge base, pre-reading activities can enhance the use of this strategy. The book introduction should include a walk-through of the book, discussion of background concepts, and a vocabulary introduction. The walk-through, or picture walk, is modified depending on the level of text being read. At the *emergent* levels, the teacher would show students the entire book, discussing each page. It is at these reading levels that the pictures and text match most closely, so understanding the pictures will be helpful in accessing the meaning strategy. At the *early* text levels, where pictures are important but there is more text, the walk-through would consist of the pictures, but less time should be spent on them. At the *fluency* levels, the pictures merely enhance the text, so teachers often ask the students to skim through the text independently or omit the walk-through.

Activating background knowledge and teaching key concepts can enhance any reading experience. If a book is concrete, or if the information in the text is not dependent upon an understanding of unfamiliar concepts, then the introduction can be as simple as saying the book is about bicycles. On the other hand, if the text requires readers to understand how people lived in the 1800s, you would need to find out what your students know about this time period and fill in any gaps in their knowledge. At the emergent and early levels, comprehension is not as dependent on background information as at the fluency levels and beyond.

Vocabulary introduction is important at all reading levels but is handled in different ways. For emergent and some early level books, pointing out vocabulary words as the child walks through the text is enough. The words in these books are generally in students' oral vocabularies, so you don't need to teach their meanings. Rather, you are showing students how a word they know looks in print. However, some books require direct teaching of words that are unfamiliar and not easily understood from context or picture clues, such as difficult names or technical words. You might choose to put these words on index cards with a sentence using the word on the back. Students benefit from some practice with unfamiliar words that are crucial for comprehension before they read them in the text. At the fluency levels, only those words which are difficult and essential to the text should be pre-taught.

In summary, the meaning cueing strategy is best taught during the oral reading of the book, but a good introduction to the book can help students use that strategy as they read. Reading to students on various topics can also enhance their background knowledge.

CUEING STRATEGY: STRUCTURE

The structure cueing strategy refers to the use of the language structure to read words. Effective use of this strategy depends on a child's understanding of the structure of the English language. Students who speak in dialect or have a limited understanding of English may find this strategy challenging and need extra support. The structure strategy is also related to meaning because at this early age, children are not able to determine the parts of speech or incorrect grammar. They just know that the word doesn't make sense from their experience with the language. Again, this strategy is best taught in the context of oral reading. Some other activities that might enhance children's understanding of language structure include the following:

Hide-a-Word. During a shared or guided reading of a text, put a piece of paper over a word in each sentence. Ask students to tell what word could be used here. Put their selection into the reading of the sentence to see if it makes sense to them. Then remove the paper to see if they correctly identified the word. We are looking for language structure sense, which cannot really be separated from meaning. This activity is sometimes referred to as *oral cloze*.

Nonsense Sentences. Create nonsense sentences such as "The dog quickly for his food" or "John borrowed the running for the afternoon." Read one sentence at a time and ask the children what is wrong in the sentence. The children respond, and you evaluate their responses. This activity could be in a game format.

CUEING STRATEGY: VISUAL (GRAPHO-PHONIC)

The visual cueing strategy includes the use of phonics—the sound-symbol relationship (i.e., we look at letters and interpret the appropriate sounds). The visual cueing strategy is more complex to teach than the others. In order for this strategy to be useful to students, they must learn the various phonemes and spelling patterns, be able to substitute letters for words with a pattern to come up with new words, and understand sound segmenting. The student needs to be able to break apart the sounds of a word and blend the sounds of the word together. The student then needs to hold the meaning of the text while reading and applying these sounds. It can take a couple of years for children to learn this strategy.

Some of the understandings stated earlier can help a student learn more easily, such as teaching phonics with whole words and focusing on spelling patterns or phonic clusters instead of individual sounds or phonic generalizations. It is also known that students learn beginning and ending sounds first, then vowel sounds. They first associate the sounds with individual letters, and then they learn phonic clusters.

The assessments in this book utilize the research and assess the students at the appropriate time and in the appropriate manner. The vowel patterns or phonic clusters are assessed in grade 2, which is an appropriate expectation. Just as the assessments evaluate the students' understandings of the sound-symbol system, the instruction and practice should follow similar formats.

Language Segmentation Activities

Language segmentation awareness is crucial to word learning and understanding the sound-symbol system. Word segmentation is the ability to distinguish the words in sentences, while syllable segmentation is the ability to distinguish syllables in words. Sound segmenting is the ability to separate the sounds in one-syllable words. This segmenting is performed orally without the visual aids of words or sentences. Have the students use markers to show the segments similar to the assessment procedure.

✳ Word Segmentation Activities

Clapping Words. Clap out the words in sentences, poetry, or songs.

Marking Words. Use blocks or markers to symbolize words. As you read a sentence, move one marker forward for each word read. Later, students can use individual sets of markers and move one for each word they hear in a sentence.

✳ Syllable Segmentation Activities

Clapping Syllables. Clap out the syllables in words (two- to three-syllable words).

Marking Syllables. Use blocks or markers to symbolize syllables. As you read a word, move one marker forward for each syllable. Later, students can use individual sets of markers and move one for each syllable they hear in a word.

✳ Sound Segmentation Activities

Marking Sounds. Use blocks or markers to symbolize sounds. Show the sounds in one-syllable, phonetically regular words by moving a marker forward for each

sound as you say it. Words chosen for this activity need to have regular patterns in them in order for students to learn the association. For example, it is not as easy to distinguish the sounds in the word *sheep* as in the word *plant* because of the digraph *sh*. Therefore, for sound segmenting practice, use one-syllable words with short and long vowels and no digraphs.

Letter-Sound Boxes. As students are writing, use boxes to help them form the word so they know how many sounds a word has, which relates to how many letters a word has, and helps develop the sound/symbol correspondence. (See Clay [1993b], pp. 32–35, and Murray & Lesniak's [1999] activity on letterboxes for more specific information.)

✳ Phonics Activities

Finding Initial and Ending Sounds. For students who are learning their initial and final sounds, it is important to provide plenty of practice identifying these sounds in words. Traditional worksheets, where a picture is given and the student must write the initial or final sound, are appropriate. You can also use book vocabulary in an activity in which the sounds are left off the words. Pronounce the word, and students write in the sound(s). (For example, for __ anket, you say: *blanket*, and students write in *bl*.)

Word Family Fill-ins. Take a word family and write it several times in a column, leaving off the initial sounds. Ask students to add letters to the beginning of the word family to create real words.

> Example:
> _____ at
> _____ at
> _____ at

Word Family Flash. Create word cards for a word family, such as *boat, float, moat, coat, bloat, goat*. Show the cards one at a time to students. Say the word and ask which letters make which sounds, saying the word again slowly and separating the initial sound from the word family, for instance, /g/ then /oat/. Then, ask students to read the word again.

Daily Word Exercise (DWE). This activity can be done with the whole class, small groups or individuals and it develops several phonics skills.

> Step 1: Select appropriate words (words from reading which are basically phonetically regular). Appropriate words for your class or group would be those that the majority of students would *not* know (are not able to read).

> Step 2: Write one of the words on the board. Ask children if they see any small parts, words, or syllables within the word that they already know. If they do, underline them and have students pronounce those particular parts.

Ask children who know the word not to pronounce it yet.

Step 3: Underline the phonetic sound parts of the word. For example, underline blends, digraphs, vowel combinations, and affixes.

Step 4: Begin at the beginning of the word and sound out the parts of the word, asking children to help you designate what the sounds of those underlined phonic elements are. After the word has been completely broken up into its sound parts, have the entire class repeat all of the sounds in sequence.

Step 5: The children as a class should be able to blend the sound elements together to form the correct word. Once the children are able to pronounce the word, the meaning should be briefly discussed, and the word should be placed within an oral sentence.

This activity takes five to ten minutes, and I usually select two words for each session.

Example of DWE with the word *sunflower*:

Write word on board: *sunflower*

Teacher: Please don't say this word if you know it. Does anyone see a part that they know?

Child: *Sun.*

Teacher: Yes, that is *sun.* (underlines word on board) Does anyone see another part in this word?

No response, so proceed to Step 3

Teacher: What about these letters? (underlines *fl*) What do these two letters say?

Child: /fl/

Teacher: Yes. (continues through sound parts of *ow* and *er*. Sometimes teacher needs to give sounds.)

Teacher: Let's say all these sounds together. (Teacher and children say /sun/, /fl/, /ow/, /er/) Who can put all the sounds together and tell me the word? Jessica?

Jessica: Sunflower.

Teacher: Yes, let's all say it together. (all say *sunflower*) One more time.

☑ Oral Fluency

Oral fluency is the effortless, smooth reading of text or easy, clear expression of ideas (Harris & Hodges, 1995). Fluency involves three components of the reading process: decoding, comprehension, and attention (Samuels, Schermer, & Reinking, 1992). Good readers use the cueing strategies automatically, understand what they read, and are focused on the text. Automaticity is achieved through much practice, often taking the form of repeated readings. Allington (2001) suggests that the lack of oral fluency in some students may be due to the inappropriate instruction received or the lack of instruction in self-monitoring skills and strategies. Stahl and Kuhn (2002) believe that the keys to developing fluency are assisted repeated reading and appropriate text level. That is, simple text or familiar text is helpful to use for the repeated readings. In addition to repeated readings, the teacher needs to support the child in the rereadings so that the cueing strategies are learned to the automatic level.

Factors That Influence Oral Fluency

- amount of oral reading practice, especially with familiar text
- automaticity of cueing strategies
- sight vocabulary knowledge

ORAL FLUENCY ACTIVITIES

Repeated Reading. All types of repeated readings are helpful. Some examples are reading together or choral reading. You will need to support students as they read by prompting them to use various cueing strategies when they make an error or get stuck on an unfamiliar word. (See cueing strategies information.)

Rereading Familiar Books. Have students reread familiar books on a regular basis in guided reading. These books can be books read in shared reading or guided reading. An objective for each guided reading instruction unit needs to be that all students are fluent with the book and can individually read it fluently to you.

Reading Plays. Primary students enjoy reading plays, and they are a good experience for developing oral fluency and verbal expression. Plays can be found at all reading levels.

Using Easy Text. An important consideration for developing oral fluency is the text level. When children are experiencing difficulty with their present level of text and need to work on fluency, using books at lower levels of difficulty is a good way to begin. After students have gotten fluent with the simpler texts, then gradually move them into more difficult text until you reach the current instructional level.

Replaying Taped Stories. Have students listen to taped stories and then imitate what they heard. Some students may need to listen to a few pages of the text at a time and then reread them on their own. A variation is for you to read a page and then have the student reread it. This continues throughout the book.

☑ Word Study

Word study focuses on two aspects of acquiring words: sight vocabulary, or words automatically pronounced without decoding, and conceptual or technical content vocabulary development. Sight vocabulary is a key player in oral fluency. In order for words to become part of their sight vocabulary, students need lots of practice so they can easily recall the specifics of these words (Ehri, 1994). Words frequently read seem to become sight vocabulary more easily than infrequently read words, so books that have repetitive words in them are helpful (Johnston, 1998). Since many teachers use predictable text and/or text with words that often are not seen again until several books later, Johnston (1998) did a study on what might influence word learning when using trade books as opposed to controlled vocabulary books. Johnston found that words needed to be identified in context by the teacher pronouncing them and the students looking for them without the aid of pictures. An example of how to do this is to create sentence strips from the text. Words should also be taught in isolation, such as in word banks.

As readers develop, almost all words will become sight vocabulary or words that are automatically read without decoding. As an adult, most words are automatic and do not require decoding. If students have difficulty learning words from reading, the reading is often choppy and disfluent.

Developing conceptual vocabulary is important for content-area learning. At the primary level, students are just beginning to develop the ability to understand conceptual vocabulary. Winters (2001) suggests that instruction build on prior knowledge and then connect, relate, or link the new information to the old. Primary students need to learn this way of studying so they can develop their skills in acquiring new information and applying it in other contexts.

Factors That Influence Word Study

- experiences with language and the world
- English language ability
- auditory memory ability
- visual memory ability

WORD STUDY ACTIVITIES

Sentence Scramble. To help students practice sight vocabulary, write sentences from a current guided reading book on sentence strips. Have students read the sentence strips and then cut them up into words. Challenge them to scramble them and put them back into the correct order.

Sight-Word Match-Up. To help develop sight vocabulary, cover up some sight words on each page of a familiar book; write the words on index cards. Read the sentence, skipping the word, and then ask students to choose the correct word from the index cards.

Word Banks. To build students' sight vocabulary, have them create individual word banks for words they don't know. Write target words on index cards and work with students on them in several ways; students need many multisensory experiences with words to know them well. You can have students write the words on paper three times each and say the word as they write. You can show students the shape of the word, word parts, or phonic clusters (spelling patterns) to help them remember the word. You can flash the words to a student and record which words are said quickly and correctly. Once a student can say a word quickly and correctly on three different dates, put it in the "known" pile and add a new word.

Sight-Word Readers. For students who have considerable trouble developing sight vocabulary, you can try sight-word readers, short text that contains many sight words. If your school has old basal readers (published before the late 1980s), you can use these as a resource. Or you can make your own or purchase some decodable texts available commercially. Have students read in their sight-word readers once or twice a week until their sight vocabulary develops. Have them read the books orally and repeatedly, until the reading is fluent. Controlled readers have limited use for developing comprehension or cueing strategies, so it's important that students have many experiences with other types of text. But the repetitiveness of sight words in these readers can really help students develop their sight vocabularies.

Sight-Word Concentration. Create a sight-word concentration game by preparing a set of cards with two of each target sight word. Shuffle the cards and place them facedown on the table. Students take turns turning over the cards and saying the words. If the words match, the student keeps the cards and gets another turn. The student with the most cards wins the game. You can adapt the game to give students practice with the words they need.

Spelling Words/Dictated Sentences. You can use word bank words as spelling words, giving students extra practice. Assess the words by saying sentences that contain them and having students write them down.

Spelling/Word Study Practice: Show a student a word bank card (from his or her individual word bank). Have him or her read the word and then spell it aloud while looking at the card. Have the student repeat the word and then write the word on the board or paper, without looking at the word. Have the student use the word bank card to check the written word. If correct, move on to the next word. If incorrect, have the student repeat the process.

Word Family Cards. Make up word family cards for a word family under study. Show a card to students. Then ask, "What sounds does (phonetic cluster) make?" Continue through other letters in the word. Then have students say the word. For example, if the word family under study is *–at*, your cards might be *cat, fat, hat, mat, pat, rat,* and *sat.* For each card, you would say, "What sound does *a t* make?" (Students would respond /at/.) "What sound does *c* make?" (Student would respond /k/.) "What is the word?" Repeat for each card, and work through the cards until students learn the words.

Word Family Chart. Make up a word family chart with blanks for beginning letters (for example, _____ ing). Have students complete the chart as you read words in the word family. Then have students reread the words and use them in sentences.

Word Hunts. Ask students to find their word bank words in a text, such as a familiar book or one at their independent reading level.

Word Anchors. An activity for developing concept vocabulary is Word Anchors (Winters, 2001). Draw a sailboat with an anchor and write the word in the bottom of the boat. Ask students for another word that might be like this word. For example: for *hurricanes,* another word could be *thunderstorms.* Next ask how the two terms are different and similar. Write these down next to the sails (+ for similar; ~ for different). Students create a way in which they will remember this word and what it means.

Contraction Concentration. An activity for contractions instruction is to write a contraction on one card and the two words for the contraction on another. Put all cards facedown and play a game of concentration, where the students have to match the contraction with the two words for it. Before this game is played, students need to know the concept of contractions and be familiar with the words used in the game.

Prefix and Suffix Matching. Give students extra practice with prefixes and suffixes by having them match the affix with its meaning either on cards or a worksheet.

Build-a-Word. Building new words from a base word is another activity that helps students develop their understanding of prefixes and suffixes. Write a base word on an index card, and then write appropriate affixes on separate cards. Take a base word, such as *call,* and add a prefix, such as *re,* to it. Ask the child what the new word is and what it means. Ask the child to use it in a sentence.

Check the Ending. You can teach inflectional endings by having children add on endings to verbs, either orally or with index cards. Worksheets in which children supply the appropriate word with the ending are also useful.

In summary, this chapter provided you with numerous techniques and activities for developing word recognition, a critical skill in the early years of learning to read. In the next chapter, we look at activities that can enhance comprehension or the main focus of reading: making meaning.

☑ Parent Home Activities for Word Recognition

Many of the following activities are done with a read aloud book; you will want to use age-appropriate books on your child's reading level. Be sure to follow suggestions from the classroom teacher.

Word Study. After you have read a book aloud to your child, ask him/her to point out three to five words that he/she knows. Put these words on index cards and flash them to your child. If he/she has trouble with any words, say the word and ask him/her to repeat it to you. Then, try flashing the words again.

Now, ask your child to select three to five words he/she does not know. Put these words on index cards. Say the words and then flash the cards. Practice the ones your child has trouble with several times. Review these cards another day to be sure they have been learned.

Poetry Read Aloud. Children in grades K–2 require practice in oral fluency, which means reading aloud with meaning. Practice in this area can easily be done with simple, rhythmic, rhyming poems. Find an anthology of children's poems and select short, simple poems to read together first, and then let your child read them alone, helping him/her with words he/she stumbles on. Repeat the reading of the poem until your child can read it alone with expression.

Repeated Readings. To increase your child's fluency and confidence while reading, either select a patterned book from the library or use a small book sent home by the teacher that your child has already read in school. First, read the whole book aloud with your child. Then go back and reread the book page by page. Children usually like it when a parent reads one page and they read the next. Switching back and forth allows them to hear more expressive reading. After reading back and forth, ask your child to read it a third time on his/her own to you.

Flash Vocabulary Practice. The purpose of this activity is to increase the reading vocabulary of your child. Collect word lists from your child's teacher. Select five to seven words to work on at a time. Put each word on an index card (3-by-5 cards work best). Show each individual card for about 15 seconds. Then turn it over. If your child did not say the correct word, show him/her the word and say it. Have your child repeat it three times while he/she slides his/her finger under the word. Put the word card back into the pile. Repeat these steps with the other words. Then flash the cards one final time to determine which words can be read.

On the back of each card write down a note to describe how your child read the words: M = mastered or read the word the first time without a problem; N = needed help in reading the word. The next time you work with these words see how many your child remembers from the N words. Then show them five to seven new words. This activity can be used all year to keep your child learning vocabulary.

Chapter 13

Intervention Instruction for Comprehension

Comprehension, or getting meaning from text, is the ultimate purpose of reading. We learn new things from reading. We get enjoyment and satisfaction from reading. It is one of the most important activities a human can do. Understanding what we read is a complex process involving the expert application of myriad strategies. In grades K–2, we introduce students to this process by emphasizing that reading should always make sense and by teaching strategies that help students get meaning from what they are reading.

Some of the first important research related to comprehension came from schema theory (Anderson & Pearson, 1984). This research revealed that expert readers use their background knowledge or prior knowledge as a basis for understanding text. Additional research has helped us understand the strategies involved in comprehension. These strategies include:

- connecting what we know to the unknown.
- monitoring our comprehension as we read.
- adjusting our understanding once we see that it is faulty.
- distinguishing important and less important details as we read.
- synthesizing information across texts.
- drawing inferences.
- asking questions while reading.

(Pearson, Roeher, Dole, & Duffy, 1992)

McLaughlin (2003) includes these strategies in her instructional model in addition to previewing, self-questioning, making connections, visualizing, knowing how words work, monitoring, summarizing, and evaluating.

Moreover, Cooper (1993) strongly advocates that reading and writing be taught together because reading and writing skills develop in tandem. Therefore, having students respond in writing to text they read is effective in promoting the development of reading comprehension. Furthermore, Taylor (1992) maintains that helping students understand text structure in terms of language patterns supports the development of comprehension. The language patterns commonly found in primary texts are:

◆ **time order**, which develops a story line in chronological order, such as a historical account;

◆ **listing**, which explains or describes one topic, such as flowers, through a series of facts and details;

◆ **compare/contrast**, which categorizes the similarities and differences between two items;

◆ **cause/effect**, which gives reasons for an event's occurrence; and

◆ **problem/resolution**, which details a problem and describes steps taken for its resolution.

In simple text, usually there is just one pattern. As text becomes more complex, patterns will alternate depending on the author's purpose in writing.

Teaching children comprehension strategies is imperative. Dowhower (1999) cites studies that reveal that little strategy teaching is actually taking place in contemporary classrooms. Teachers are skilled at asking questions but often fail to model comprehension strategies or foster understandings that will promote efficient comprehension. Keene and Zimmermann (1997) suggest that asking students to make connections to what they're reading, to other texts, and to the larger world is essential in helping them comprehend text in a meaningful way. The next section outlines some basic understandings about comprehension to keep in mind as you create lesson plans.

✺ Basic Understandings About Teaching Comprehension

◉ Prior knowledge is related to oral language development and experiences with language and life. Our schema, prior knowledge, develops from our language development and life experiences.

◉ Strategies or process understandings are the framework of comprehension or meaning of text. If we understand how to read effectively, such as asking questions while reading or clarifying our confusions (strategies), we are more likely to have a better understanding of what we read.

◉ To get meaning from text, we need to personalize the meaning or relate personally to the text, thereby linking or connecting the new knowledge to our prior knowledge.

◉ Skills such as identifying main ideas in text provide the mechanics of comprehension and help to facilitate the use of strategies.

- Understanding the structure of language, such as knowing about pronouns and how they work as referents, provides a basis for unlocking the meanings of unfamiliar words or phrases.

- Knowledge and identification of the five structural patterns commonly found in text help readers understand the author's intent and message.

- Understanding the characteristics of various genres further enhances readers' understanding of a text and an author's purpose.

Factors That Influence Comprehension

- depth and breadth of prior knowledge
- automaticity of word recognition
- fluency of reading

 Recommended Best Practices for Comprehension

If we know all this about comprehension, then what is the best approach for teaching primary students? First of all, much of the instruction in comprehension strategies needs to be done during read aloud and shared reading. Since K–2 students are in the midst of developing their word recognition skills by reading relatively simple text with repetitive or predictable language patterns, it is more effective to model and practice comprehension skills on books above their reading level, although not above their comprehension level. They can understand these texts and apply comprehension strategies to them—they just can't decode all the words. Using this forum for teaching also allows you to select books that lend themselves to using the strategy you want to model.

A model lesson plan of instruction for comprehension would include:

1. Identifying and activating students' prior knowledge,

2. Connecting or linking that knowledge to the text,

3. Providing a reading guide of questions (oral or written) that facilitate student learning of the main elements of the text, text structure, and/or language patterns, and

4. Guiding the development of comprehension strategies so that the student becomes an independent, active reader.

Dowhower (1999) suggests a simple lesson plan format of **prereading** to develop prior knowledge and set a purpose for reading; **active reading**, in which students are actively engaged in the reading through questioning and discussion; and **post reading**, which includes independent follow-up activities.

In grades K–2, we emphasize word recognition, but we must not neglect comprehension. Primary children can learn to summarize a story with main events, ask questions about what they read, predict what they are going to read, clarify or verify their predictions, and answer questions from the text. These expectations are the start of some important concepts and understandings about comprehension.

Intervention Activities for Comprehension

The following chart lists the expectations, assessment items, and intervention activities for comprehension.

Comprehension

Kindergarten Expectations	Assessment Items	Intervention Activities
• Understand that pictures help tell the story.	KAR.5 Understands topic of book.	Comprehension: Retelling/Summarize; Fiction Text
• Understand that the book is true life or fantasy.	KBR.7 Tells details of book.	Comprehension: Detail; Nonfiction Text
• Identify the topic or theme of the book.	KCR.7 Tells details of book.	Comprehension: Detail; Nonfiction Text

Grade 1 Expectations	Assessment Items	Intervention Activities
• Rely on their knowledge of the topic they are reading to keep the reading meaningful (making connections).	1AR.5 Completes a cloze exercise.	Comprehension: Cloze; Fiction Text
	1BR.2 Orally retells story.	Comprehension: Retelling/Summarize; Fiction Text
• Able to retell and summarize reading.	1BR.4 Completes a cloze exercise.	Comprehension: Cloze
• Complete cloze sentences, which indicates understanding of story sentence structure.	1CR.2 Retells book in writing.	Comprehension: Retelling/Summarize; Fiction Text Writing: Mechanics
• Develop an understanding of text structures, such as sequence and description.	1CR.3 Completes a cloze exercise.	Comprehension: Cloze
• Begin to identify story elements, such as problem and resolution.		
• Understand the difference between fiction and nonfiction.		
• Understand some genres including biography, folk tale, fairy tale, informational article, and poetry.		
• Utilize silent reading.		

Grade 2 Expectations	Assessment Items	Intervention Activities
• Develop an understanding of literary elements, including title, author, genre, plot, climax, characters, and problem/resolution. • Understand some of the elements of nonfiction text (format, content, graphics). • Develop an understanding of fact versus opinion. • Begin to interpret or make connections with the text read and infer. • Identify main ideas in text. • Identify the author's purpose for writing. • Recall details of text. • Understand how to use the text and own experiences to make connections. • Develop an understanding of text structures: time order, description, compare/contrast, cause/effect, and problem/resolution.	2AR.2 Retells story in writing.	Comprehension: Retelling/Summarize; Fiction Text Writing: Mechanics
	2BR.1 Silently reads text and writes a brief summary.	Comprehension: Retelling/Summarize; Fiction Text Writing: Mechanics
	2BR.2 Identifies problem of story and ways to solve problem.	Comprehension: Problem/Resolution Writing: Mechanics
	2BR.3 Completes a cloze exercise without using book.	Comprehension: Cloze
	2CR.1 Silently reads text and responds to questions.	Comprehension: Detail; Finding Facts; Nonfiction Text Writing: Mechanics

☑ Cloze Activities

The cloze format helps determine a student's ability to process text. In order to complete a cloze exercise, a student must read the words, understand the meaning of words, and understand the structure of the English language. Cloze activities provide an opportunity for students to practice cueing strategies and use context clues and language structure. In addition, cloze exercises are easy to create and evaluate. For these reasons, they can be a beneficial tool in evaluating and planning reading instruction.

ORAL CLOZE IN A SHARED READING SETTING

Prerequisite: Story has been read by teacher and student at least once

For kindergarten or first-grade children, this activity works well to introduce them to the cloze format before they experience written exercises. Reread a familiar story with the children, preferably in Big Book format. Next, cover some target words with sticky notes. At first, cover no more than one word per sentence, and just a few words per story. Choose words that students can figure out based on their knowledge of language structure or context clues. For the sentence, *Sally wanted to get a present for her mother because it was her birthday*, the words that would be easily identified when covered up by a sticky note are *present*, *mother*, and *birthday*. The words *her*, *because*, and *was* would be more difficult for a young child to identify or remember from the text.

Once you've covered the target words, reread the story. When you come to a covered word, say "blank" and read to the end of the sentence. Then return to the sentence and reread it, stopping at the blank. Ask students what word would make sense in the blank. Take suggestions and reread the sentence with the suggested word. Then ask students if the word makes sense. If it does make sense, ask what letter we would expect to see at the beginning of the word. Uncover the word and have children check their answers. If the word makes sense in the sentence but turns out to be a synonym, ask why it cannot be that word. This reinforces the idea that text must be meaningful *and* fit the visual representation in order for it to be correct. Repeat until the story is finished. Keep in mind that in the beginning, only a few words are covered; once children learn the procedures, you can cover more words.

Activity time: 10–15 minutes per session.

SIMPLE CLOZE FROM TEXT

Prerequisite: Story has been read by student

In the primary grades or for students with limited English proficiency, a simple cloze exercise from the text is useful. Select sentences from a text students have read before and write them on a worksheet or chart paper, leaving out words that are meaningful to the context of the story. First, leave out one word per sentence, then leave out two words in more complex sentences. Be careful not to leave out words that could be replaced by any word. Selecting appropriate words is most difficult in simpler texts. For example, if the text read: *I found some oranges*, a reader could take out *oranges* and replace it with any object and be correct. He or she could even select another word from the text and be correct, such as *bananas* (page 2 of text read: *I found some bananas.*). Therefore, a more appropriate word to leave out is *found*, or you could select a different sentence with more context-dependent words. In more complex text, such as *The princess went into the castle to see her father the king*, the words *castle*, *princess*, or *father* could each be used as the take-out word.

Start with three to five sentences until students understand the exercise. For first graders, eight to ten sentences seems to be the limit, while second-grade children can usually complete about ten to fifteen sentences, depending on the reading level. It is helpful to start out with a few sentences and then increase the number of them. Also, not all sentences lend themselves to this exercise.

Activity time: 10–15 minutes per session.

CLOZE FROM MEANING OF TEXT

Prerequisite: Story has been read by student

Another approach used with students who are reading more complex text is to develop sentences based on the meaning of the text but not taken directly from the text. Students must be fluent readers who can decode well, since the text is unfamiliar. In addition, the student has to remember the meaning of the text read in detail so he or she can fill in the blanks with the appropriate words.

The other aspects of developing this cloze are similar to the Simple Cloze activity. First, leave out one word per sentence, then leave out two words in more complex sentences. Be careful not to leave out words which could be replaced by any word. Remember that any word which makes sense in the sentence and is within the meaning of the story is acceptable.

Activity time: 10–15 minutes per session.

UNRELATED CLOZE EXERCISES

Prerequisites: Integration of cueing strategies and fluency of reading

This cloze exercise is the most difficult of the three written types because the student has not read a story that relates to the exercise. Many teachers purchase commercial cloze activities for this exercise, which is a good practice. The purpose of this exercise is to help students practice strategies for approaching unfamiliar words. Make sure that the reading level of the cloze exercise does not exceed the student's ability to fluently read the material. Be sure to select easy reading materials in the beginning and then increase the difficulty when the strategies have been learned.

Gather a small group of readers at similar reading levels and follow this procedure:

1. Read the title together and have children brainstorm what the text could be about.

2. Have one student read aloud the first sentence of the text. Is it a topic sentence? What will the rest of the sentences be about? Brainstorm ideas and write them down on a chart.

3. Ask students to read the paragraph silently, supplying whatever word comes to their heads for the blanks they encounter. If you're using a commercial program that supplies a word bank, have students cover up the

choices. Then discuss and compare the ideas they suggested before reading to the ideas that were really in the selection.

4. Have students share the words they came up with for the blanks. Take each suggestion and reread it in the sentence. Ask if it makes sense and uncover the word bank to see if it is a choice. If it is not a choice given, ask them which choice comes closest to this one.

5. Continue with this process through the paragraphs. As students become adept at supplying words, have them read more of the text silently until they can read the entire passage without support.

6. After the students are able to read the passage independently without support, correct the exercise individually so that you can use the same process above (step 4) on the individual errors of the students. Students will learn more readily if their needs and instruction are congruent.

Activity time: 20–30 minutes per session.

☑ Retelling/Summarizing Activities

Retelling is the first step toward teaching students how to write summaries. A retelling has many more details than a summary, but students need to understand the concept of telling about what they read in their own words before they can begin writing summaries.

Retelling Read Alouds. To introduce the concept of retelling, retell stories you've read aloud. When you finish a book, put it down and say, "Now I'd like to retell the story, to make sure I can remember it and talk about it. In the beginning,[retell story]." You can chart the story as you retell and ask students to contribute details. Be sure to discuss beginning, middle, and end. Once you've done this several times, invite students to retell a read aloud collaboratively. If students have a hard time with the retelling after reading, you can scaffold their learning by retelling the story as you read it. Stop at key points in the story and model retelling just that piece of the story.

Find the Beginning, Middle, and End. Once students can retell a story, you can model summary writing. Explain that students need to think of a general statement or statements to describe the main idea, instead of simply including all the details for the beginning, middle, and end. Modeling with a read aloud story initially helps students grasp the concept. Then you can have students summarize guided reading books so you can support them in a small group setting. Finally, have students practice summarizing independently.

Main Idea Match-Up. Helping students learn how to identify the main idea of passages makes summarizing easier. For this fun activity, select short passages that have a clear main idea; the passages can be fiction or nonfiction. Write down the main idea for each passage on an index card. Put the main ideas in front of the children. Read aloud the passages one at a time and have the students select the appropriate main idea. When students are proficient with this activity, you can have students do it individually. In the most advanced version, students can read the passages on their own (passages must be at their instructional reading level) and select the main idea.

Just-Right Summaries. Sometimes students either write too much in a summary, or they leave out key parts. This activity helps students include just the right amount of information. Write three versions of a summary of a familiar story (folk tales work well) on index cards. One version is "just right," summarizing the beginning, middle, and end. One has "too much detail," and one has "left out parts." Children read the index cards to themselves and tell which category each summary falls under; have them discuss their reasons. Provide support and feedback until students can perform the task independently. Once they've mastered it, students can try their hand at writing their own summaries.

Sum It Up Story Map. Students can begin to understand story elements by using a story map, a graphic organizer that has spaces for writing in the title, author, characters, setting, and plot events. The plot events are usually done in a beginning, middle, and end format. The story map helps children express the main ideas in each of these parts of the story. (See Appendix for Literary Elements Chart.)

☑ Oral Language Activities (Grades K and 1)

If children come to school with inadequate oral language skills, comprehending text that they are listening to is often difficult. Second Language Learners are often at risk with oral language skills. In these cases, building oral language skills during guided reading time can be helpful in developing comprehension. Here are some activities which can help develop these skills.

Listen and Learn. This easy activity builds children's knowledge of language structures and patterns. Select straightforward picture books with only one to three lines of print per page. The text needs to have simple language and common vocabulary in order for students to incorporate it into their own language. Repetitive text or text that rhymes also works well. These books can be on tape or you or another adult can read them aloud. Students will each need their own copy of the book. For the first reading, you will probably need to assist the students with the listening. As you read or play the tape, help students follow along and turn the pages at the appropriate time. Ask students to point to the words as they listen. Children can then reread the book with the tape or with you until they are proficient with following and keeping up with the reader.

Chime In. Once children are familiar with a text, you can ask them to repeat some of the sentences in the book. As you're reading, stop after a sentence—one that's interesting or has some key vocabulary in it—and ask students to repeat it. Say it along with them a few times, helping them read with expression and understanding.

Picture Talk. After rereading a text a few times, show a picture to students from the book and have them tell what is happening at that point in the story. Ask if it's at the beginning, middle, or end; what the characters are doing; what the problem is. This kind of quick discussion introduces them to the language of a story and helps them get comfortable talking and thinking about text.

Literacy Play Centers. Set up play centers that focus on real-world experiences, such as a post office, grocery store, library, or restaurant, to build students' background knowledge and increase their vocabulary. Include items appropriate to the service, such as letters, stamps, and mailboxes for the post office. Model how the service operates and act out various roles the students could play at the center. Then allow students to play and interact with each other, supporting their oral language use by supplying words and phrases they might need to communicate.

Nursery Rhyme Act-Outs. Nursery rhymes appeal to children and can be easily acted out while saying the rhyme. Short, simple, rhythmic poems can also be used. The movements help make the text concrete for students, thereby aiding comprehension. First, copy the rhyme on chart paper and read it with students several times, pointing to the words as you go. Then, demonstrate the body movements for each part. Invite children to follow along, reading the rhyme and doing the movements. Once students get the hang of it, they can practice on their own and then perform for the class.

Say a Sentence. For those students who have difficulty speaking in sentences, this activity can help them develop an awareness of sentence structures. Select sentences that you want children to repeat. Begin with sentences that are slightly more involved than what the children are presently speaking. For example, if a child is speaking with only phrases (*want cookie*), you might begin with simple sentences with a subject and predicate (*I want a cookie.*). Then you can slowly increase the complexity and length of the sentences over time. Base the sentences for instruction on the student's own language use of incorrect sentences or just phrases. Relating the sentence repetition to his/her own language will be meaningful. You can also use sentences from books read to or by him/her.

Find the Answer Game. Create eight to ten question-and-answer card sets. Choose questions that are of interest to students or relate to the curriculum. Write the question on one card and the answer on another. Be sure to illustrate the answer card. Spread out the answer cards so all players can see them. Then invite the first player to select a question card. Read the question and ask the player to choose the card that answers it. Then have the player answer orally in a complete sentence. If the answer is correct, the student gets to keep the card and take another turn. If the student answers correctly again, the next player goes. Correctness is determined by two things: appropriateness of the response to the question and the language structure of the response. If your students have major difficulties in speaking complete grammatical sentence responses, you might want to start with appropriate content and some sentence structure correctness and work toward the goal of having both be correct. The players only get a maximum of two chances per turn. This rule helps keep the game moving and allows all children to practice their skills. The winner is the player holding the most cards.

Draw and Tell a Story. Help students build their oral language and comprehension skills by creating their own stories. Invite students to choose a topic and tell a story about it in pictures. Have them draw one picture per page and at least three pictures per story. Then have them tell the story to you orally. As they tell it, write down what they say. At first, encourage students to tell one sentence per illustration, working up to more sentences and more detail over time. If the child uses incorrect language structure, repeat the sentence with correct language structure and write it on the paper that way.

Once the story is complete, have the child practice reading the story with you. Please remember that the purpose is not to teach the child how to read the words, but rather to hear the appropriate language structures. Therefore, always read the sentences while the child turns the pages and reads along.

Movement Songs/Finger Plays. Songs and finger plays are fun activities that enhance oral language development. Students can learn and perform songs such as the "Hokey, Pokey" and finger plays such as "Isty Bitsy Spider." These types of activities help the children associate the language with the movement.

☑ Fiction Text Activities

Rewrite the Book. Rewriting books is an important comprehension activity that helps students relate to text structure. For kindergarten and first grade, it can be an excellent activity for not only comprehension, but for writing as well. Not all books lend themselves to rewriting; repetitive and rhythmic books that are simple seem to work best. Prepare a book modeled after one they've recently read. For instance, after students have read *I Like Fruit*, you can prepare a series of pages

with the sentence, *I like* _____. Students put a word in the blank and draw a picture to correspond to the word. The word will probably be written in unconventional spelling. Children can then read these books to others.

Whole-Class Rewrite. Another way to rewrite books is to have the whole class rewrite a book together. Folktales are a good resource for this kind of class writing. Guide students to choose new characters, new plot events, and new vocabulary, keeping the overall theme of the story the same. For example, with *Little Red Riding Hood* the story might become *Little Gray Squirrel*. The squirrel goes off to the grandmother squirrel's house and the villain is a fox. This type of rewriting provides a great opportunity to talk about literary elements, too.

Think Alouds (Grade 2 or higher for student participation). Think Alouds help readers engage with text and monitor their comprehension. Developing active readers is the key goal in this activity. Oster (2001) describes it as verbalizing your thoughts as you read. Oster suggests four strategies to focus on during this activity: verifying, retelling, rereading, and reading on to clarify. Students are instructed to write down what they are thinking as they read. They are also taught the four strategies to practice as they are reading. At the primary level, we can introduce students to the idea of the Think Aloud by modeling it during Read Aloud and shared reading and inviting students to participate. To model verifying, for instance, you might pause and say, "Hmmm. I'm going to think aloud here about a problem I'm having understanding the story. On this page, I just read that Max is playing on the swing with his sister. But I thought he had invited his friend Marc. I'm going to go back and reread the page before this to verify that he invited Marc. Before I do that, does anyone remember what happened to Marc?" Through their contributions, you can evaluate students' basic knowledge, vocabulary, literal comprehension, understanding of literary devices, ability to relate new information to old, and ability to make inferences and predictions.

DRTA: Directed Reading Thinking Activity. Dowhower (1999). This technique can be utilized with either narrative or expository text. In this activity, students predict what they think the book will be about by looking at the title, table of contents, pictures, and other text features. They read a section of the text and verify if their predictions were correct. They predict again. They read and verify again. This cycle continues throughout the text.

Rich Read Alouds. Reading Aloud can be an excellent tool for developing comprehension strategies and skills. Beck & McKeown (2001) support reading to students to foster quality talk about books. Select texts that will challenge students but not turn them off. It can be a complex text with new concepts, as long as students will be interested in the topic and motivated to listen. Discuss the book as you read it aloud, but do not show any illustrations (this keeps students focused on the text). Ask open-ended questions that encourage students to make inferences and connections, and follow-up questions that help them elaborate on their thinking. After you've read through and students have talked about the text, you can show the illustrations. At this time, present two to four rich words for vocabulary instruction. Present the words in the context of the story, but provide additional scenarios in which the words might be used. Then challenge students to use the words in sentences of their own.

ETR: Experience-Text-Relationship. Dowhower (1999). This technique is primarily used with narrative text. The reader's background experiences and schema are linked to the story content before, during, and after the text is read. Before reading, discuss the content of the text and provide instruction for any confusions. During reading, ask questions at appropriate places to ensure that students are connecting. Finally, after reading, support students in making connections to the text.

Story Structure Web. Dowhower (1999). Help students develop their awareness of story elements by creating a web (or chart) and having students fill it in with information from the text. You can include characters, setting, plot, genre, and climax on the chart (depending on your teaching focus and students' needs). Guide students to talk through their reasoning to build their understanding of these important concepts. This technique works well with narrative text, but can be used with expository text as well.

Visualize This. Dowhower (1999) recommends using graphic organizers, story maps, concept webs, or other visual tools to represent the content of a text. Showing plot structure or other story elements visually helps students make connections and see relationships in the text.

Response Journals. Writing in response to text is an excellent way to build comprehension, and even primary students can begin to write about what they're reading in journals. This is a great way for them to make text-to-self, text-to-text, and text-to-world connections and to ask questions. In kindergarten and first grade, responses may be mostly drawings with a few labels, but second graders can be encouraged to write sentences, using invented spelling. Some prompts to get students thinking include: *What part of the book reminds you of something in your own life? What part of the book reminds you of another book? What would you have done differently from the character?*

Reading Guides. Reading guides help students practice comprehension skills and strategies. Follow these steps to create a reading guide.

1. Analyze the structure, format, and author's message for the book. This analysis is the framework for the guide.

2. Using the framework, develop the questions, graphics, or vocabulary exercises for the reader. There should be one to two questions per chapter or per main event. Sometimes the guide can be a literary elements chart, or

an outline or a graphic organizer. Remember, questions must involve higher-level thinking, interpretation, and inference which relates to the text and author's message. Students need to find text support for their answers.

3. Create questions that address the reader's experiences. These questions can be answered by using text information and personal experience.

4. Present the reading guide to students and have them complete it as they read the text. It is suggested that a chapter or section be assigned per each guided reading session. Provide feedback and support to the students as they read during the guided reading session. The students come to the session with the responses completed for that chapter. Discuss their answers to ensure that they understand the text.

Question As You Read. Writing questions while reading helps readers become more actively involved in the reading. For primary students, using sticky notes and attaching them to the text as they read can be effective. These questions can relate to unfamiliar words, predictions, personal reflections, and connections to other books. At the primary grades, model this technique by having students read a page or paragraph. Present your own question along with the students' questions. Then read the next paragraph or page and repeat the process. This demonstration can assist students in understanding the variety of questions that can be asked when one is actively reading.

☑ Nonfiction Text Activities

All of the fiction text activities (see pages 173–176) can be adapted for use with nonfiction texts. Here are a few others especially for nonfiction.

KWL: Know, What to Learn, Learned. Dowhower (1999). This technique is often used with expository text. Create a three-column chart on chart paper. Lead a class discussion on what students already know about the topic of the book, which activates their prior knowledge. Next, ask students what they would like to learn about this topic. Then read the text together. Invite students to talk about what they learned from the text and record their responses on the chart. Keep the charts for review and reference.

Book Introduction. Nonfiction text needs a special introduction for primary students who are unfamiliar with these genres. Select a nonfiction text based on students' knowledge and interests, so they can easily connect to it. Review the text carefully for special text features before sharing it with students. Note particular types of print, graphics, and other features that you want to point out to students. Demonstrate how these special print features communicate the author's message.

Teach any concepts or vocabulary necessary to better understand the content. After previewing the text and discussing format and vocabulary, invite students to predict the author's message and information they will learn from this text. After the students read the text, guide them to verify their predictions, and list what they have learned.

☑ Finding Facts Activities

Missing Fact Game. Make recalling facts fun with this engaging activity that strengthens comprehension skills.

1. Select a familiar nonfiction book that the students have read several times.

2. Rewrite three or more short passages (two to four sentences) on chart paper or index cards, leaving out one key fact from each passage.

3. Write the missing facts on index cards, one fact per card.

4. Ask students to reread the text, or read it aloud to them.

5. Select, or have the first player select, a passage to read. The player must find the missing fact from the passage on an index card. If the selection is correct, the player gets to keep the card, and the next player takes a turn. The player with the most cards wins.

Is That a Fact? When reading nonfiction during guided reading, review the definition of a fact: something which can be proven to be true or false. Then have children read one page at a time and find the facts on the page. Write the facts on chart paper and then discuss how we know they are facts.

☑ Problem/Resolution Activities

Picture Problems. Develop students' understanding of problem and resolution with this fun activity. Select pictures (from trade books, magazines, or other sources) that show problems. Then gather pictures that show how the problems were resolved. Have students match the problem with its solution. As an extension activity, have the children draw their own problem-resolution cards and have their friends match them up.

Student Solvers. Select a short, simple passage or story with a clear problem. Read it aloud, stopping at the end of the description of the problem. Ask students how it might be solved. Write their suggestions on chart paper, then continue reading to see how the author resolved the problem. Compare the author's resolution to the students' responses.

Guided Reading Problem/Resolution Activity. Select a story that has a clear problem/resolution. Mysteries and folk tales work especially well for this activity. Then create a graphic organizer with space for writing the problem, steps to resolution, and resolution. As students are reading, support and guide them to identify these three areas in the story.

☑ Detail Activities

Detail Questions Activity. As you ask comprehension questions during the reading of a text, have children read aloud the passage that supports their answers. The comprehension level of the questions will reflect the level of text being read, so if the text is literal, then most questions will be literal. But the practice of going back to the text to find details to support an answer is a sound one.

Picture Details. Help students pay attention to details with this quick and easy exercise. Select a picture with lots of details and have students list as many as they can; record their answers on chart paper. Then invite students to write a story together, incorporating as many details as possible. When students are proficient with this as a group, you can have them do it independently.

☑ Parent Home Activities for Comprehension

Many of the following activities are done with a read aloud book; you will want to use age-appropriate books on your child's reading level. Be sure to follow suggestions from the classroom teacher. (See Parent Book Selection and Reading Chart in Appendix)

Read Alouds. One of the easiest and most pleasurable activities to build comprehension is reading aloud. Select a book based on your child's interests as well as grade level.

In addition to reading the book, you will want to ask your child some questions at the end of the reading. Here are some suggestions; adapt them for the book you've read.

Type of Book	Kindergarten	Grade 1	Grade 2
Fiction or storybooks	Tell me one thing you remember from the story. Tell me what the problem was in the story. Tell me why the character did _____.	Tell me one thing that happened in the beginning. Tell me one thing that happened in the middle. Tell me one thing that happened at the end. What did you like about this book? What was the problem in this book? How did they solve the problem?	Tell me what happened in the beginning. Tell me what happened in the middle. Tell me what happened at the end. What did you like about this book? What was the problem in this book? How did they solve the problem? Tell me what the character could have done differently. Would you like to be the character and why.
Nonfiction books	Name one thing that you found interesting about the topic in the book.	What are three facts you learned about the topic?	What are some facts you learned about the topic? What more do you want to learn about the topic? Why does this topic interest you?

Ask Questions Activity. Select an appropriate read aloud book for your child. Skim through the pictures and ask your child to come up with three to five questions he or she wants to know about the book such as "Why did the lady paint her house?" or "Where do dragonflies live?" Write the questions down. Read the book to your child. Next, look at the questions and ask your child to respond based on the book read. Some questions may not have been answered, so this gives you another opportunity to read another book on the topic or imagine the answer in the case of a fiction book.

Personal Reflection Activity. This activity can be done with a read aloud book or a book your child read in school. After reading the book, ask your child to tell, make a picture, or write about
- his/her favorite part of the book and why
- what he/she would do differently than the character
- how the character could have solved the problem differently
- how he/she feels about the book
- what more he/she wants to learn about the topic of the book

Select only one or two of the ideas per book for your child. Have your child share his/her answers with you. If your child writes, be sure to give him/her help with spelling if asked. Also, just share with your child the thoughts expressed rather than worrying about editing the writing. If your child wants to know about how to improve the writing, then as a parent you can make a few suggestions, but you want to keep it positive. Enjoy these book experiences with your child.

Chapter 14

Intervention Instruction for Writing

Writing is one of the most vital aspects of the language arts. It can be fun and fulfilling if one is fluent. However, when one has difficulty with it, it can be torture. This chapter will suggest some effective methods and activities to make writing easier and more enjoyable for students.

My experiences have made clear to me that teaching reading and writing together promotes literacy faster and more effectively than teaching them separately. Cooper (1993) agrees and supports his view with research studies that have demonstrated the following reasons for keeping reading and writing instruction together:

◆ both are constructive processes,

◆ they share similar processes and draw on the same kinds of knowledge,

◆ they enhance each other when taught together, and

◆ higher-level thinking is an outcome of teaching the two together.

This chapter discusses ways in which you can instruct reading and connect it to writing in a small-group setting, such as guided reading. To begin, let's examine some factors that influence writing as it is developing in kindergarten through grade 2.

Factors That Influence Writing

◉ Knowledge of the formation of upper- and lowercase letters

◉ Ability to form the letters appropriately and fluently

◉ Knowledge of the sounds of letters and spelling patterns of words

◉ Experiences and prior knowledge base

◉ Knowledge of the mechanics of the English language

◉ Ability to imagine and be creative

◉ Vocabulary

◉ Ability to manipulate the English language

The skills and abilities students have in these areas influence their writing development, but instruction can impact it significantly. A writing-rich classroom environment is one in which writing is encouraged and taught daily, where there are structures such as writing centers, writing workshops, mini-lessons, writing conferences, and scaffolded instruction. All of these activities promote students' writing development.

☀ Learning How to Write

Learning to write involves knowledge of the mechanics of writing. First of all, the students should know how to form the letters they want to write and which ones are needed to write the words (spelling). This aspect of writing mechanics can be difficult for some children. Learning to write the letters usually happens in kindergarten. There are many different formats for learning, such as letter of the week, a commercial program, or starting with known letters such as in students' names. Whatever program is utilized, it is important that the letters become meaningful to students and that instruction follows the students' development in writing and their needs. Some ideas that have worked well for me include

- ◆ teaching the lower- and uppercase letters together;

- ◆ teaching dissimilar letters (k, p) together so children are less confused by similar configurations of letters (b, d);

- ◆ providing a visual cue to attach to the letter, such as a picture;

- ◆ writing out words for students that contain the letters they are learning; and

- ◆ providing multisensory practice in writing the letters.

Keep in mind that "correct formation" means that the letter looks like the appropriate letter; it does not mean a child must follow the prescribed way of forming a letter (e.g., using an upstroke instead of a downstroke). It may be impossible to change a stroke in writing the letter; what is most important is the legibility of the handwriting and how quickly it can be written.

In terms of spelling, we know that there is a developmental progression (Gentry, 1984; Graves, 1983). First, children write initial and final consonants to represent words. Next, they add interior consonants. Children use consonants with vowel holders until they master conventional spelling with appropriate vowels. Students rely on their knowledge of sound-symbol relationships in the early stages of writing. As they move toward conventional spelling, they begin to use the visual features of words or patterns to write.

Punctuation, capitalization, and grammar are the other mechanics that developing writers need to learn. Initially, students use their own language to write. The amount of listening to text and reading independently influences the transition to book language in writing. Students become aware that they can mimic the writing they read as well as the language they hear. Dictated sentences and daily sentence correction activities help students learn the basic mechanics. As writing becomes fluent and lengthy, more direct instruction in mechanics is necessary, through mini-lessons and conferences.

Best Practices for Teaching Writing

Students need to have a balanced approach to writing and write often. Here is a suggested format based on best practices.

1. Weekly writing sessions need to include whole-group writing, small-group writing around a text, and individual writing.

2. For kindergarten, writing instruction involves a great deal of whole-group writing that demonstrates how a piece of writing is created. In a small-group setting such as guided reading, letter formation is often a focus. For individual writing, most kindergarteners draw pictures and write some letters to represent words describing their picture.

3. For grades 1 and 2, in whole-group writing experiences, introduce students to various genres and demonstrate how to organize longer pieces. In small groups, students learn response writing and various strategies for developing writing. For individual writing, students write journal entries, stories, and essays of their own choosing. We can support students by providing word walls, dictionaries, and other easy-to-use resources as well as conferring with them individually.

4. Mechanics instruction has a different focus at each grade level. In kindergarten, students focus on learning the alphabet and being able to write letters automatically. This fluency provides the gateway into writing for the future. Students who struggle with the formation of letters tend to be reluctant to write in higher grades.

    In grade 1, students develop their writing fluency and handwriting skills. Students should be writing simple stories independently by the time they leave first grade. Spelling strategies are also a focus.

    In grade 2, students begin to edit their own work for spelling, capitalization, punctuation, and grammar. Students need direct instruction in these areas and lots of practice using what they've learned in independent writing.

 **Intervention Activities for Writing**

The following chart lists the expectations, assessment items, and intervention activities for writing.

Writing
Expectations/Assessment Items/Intervention Activities

Kindergarten Expectations	Assessment Items	Intervention Activities
• Write their first name with appropriate upper- and lowercase letters.	KAW.6 Writes name.	Writing: Alphabet
	KAW.7 Spells name.	Writing: Alphabet
• Write some letters of the alphabet.	KBW.10 Identifies letters in name and words.	Writing: Alphabet
• Identify the names of 45 out of 52 letters.	KBW.11 Draws picture to convey meaning.	Writing: Story; Mechanics
• Write some words with invented spelling and some letters that represent words such as *d* for *dad*.	KBW.12 Writes name on paper and writes letters to make words about picture.	Writing: Story; Mechanics
	KBW.13 Identifies letters.	Writing: Alphabet
	KBW.14 Writes letters.	Writing: Alphabet
	KCW.10 Draws picture to convey meaning.	Writing: Story; Mechanics
	KCW.11 Writes letters to make words about picture.	Writing: Story; Mechanics
	KCW.12 Identifies letters.	Writing: Alphabet
	KCW.13 Writes letters.	Writing: Alphabet

Grade 1 Expectations	Assessment Items	Intervention Activities
• Identify all 26 upper- and lowercase letters.	1AW.10 Writes letters of alphabet.	Writing: Alphabet
• Write simple sentences and use appropriate capitalization and punctuation.	1AW.11 Writes some response sentences.	Writing Response: Mechanics
• Write all upper- and lowercase alphabet letters.	1BW.8 Writes a simple story.	Writing: Story; Mechanics
• Write simple stories of several sentences.	1CW.7 Writes a response which has a minimum of five sentences.	Writing: Response; Mechanics
• Respond to a writing prompt, though may not include all the details.		
• Use their knowledge of phonics to spell words, but also have command of several conventional spelling words.		

Grade 2 Expectations	Assessment Items	Intervention Activities
• Attempt to organize writing and develop it fully.	2AW.4 Writes a story which includes a beginning, middle, and end. Includes adjectives.	Writing: Story; Enhancement; Mechanics
• Use more complex and varied sentence structures.	2BW.5 Writes a story with problem, steps for resolution, and a resolution.	Writing: Story; Mechanics; Genre
• Add details or words (adjectives, adverbs) to write more vividly.	2CW.2 Writes a response to the question with appropriate supporting details from the text.	Writing: Response; Mechanics
• Use predominantly conventional spelling, with invented spelling of more sophisticated words.		
• Proofread for simple sentence mechanics, such as capitals at the beginning of sentences and some proper nouns, and ending punctuation.		

☑ Alphabet Activities

Alphabet learning involves being able to identify letters, write letters, and know their sounds. The following activities focus mostly on identifying and writing letters. A discussion on teaching letter sounds can be found in Chapter 12 in the phonics section. If a student is confusing two letters, practice only one of those letters for a period of time. The confusion should clear up.

Individual Alphabet Books. Create an alphabet book with individual children. Each child selects the *A* picture for their book, *B* picture for their book, and so on. Having children choose the pictures reinforces their learning and makes it more meaningful. It is particularly useful in helping struggling learners remember letter names.

Alphabet Bingo. Create bingo cards with 5-by-5-inch grids filled with upper- and lowercase letters. You can target certain letters for specific cards to individualize learning. Hand out the cards and then begin calling letters. Have students cover up the letter if they have it (using a scrap of paper or some other marker). The traditional ways of winning can be agreed to at the beginning of the game. Winners can be the first to fill the whole card or one row/column or diagonal. It's the teacher's choice.

Say the Letter. Write isolated words and have students say the letters in the word or spell it.

Sensory Letters. Provide opportunities for students to write letters with sand, water, or paint. Have them say the letter as they write it.

Tactile Letters. Create letters out of sandpaper or clay. Have students trace over these letters and say them. Magnetic letters are also useful for spelling out words or for tracing over them and saying the letters.

Slate Writing. In the beginning stages of handwriting, students can practice letter formation on erasable slates or white boards during guided reading. Slate writing makes it easy to correct letter formation as it is being done. The slate is also a quick way to practice several times.

Say It As You Write It. For letters students are having trouble with, have them say the formation directions as they write the letters. An example of these directions would be for the letter *b*: straight down, then around. Sometimes students need a multi-sensory approach to remember the formation.

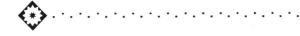

☑ Mechanics Activities

Mechanics include handwriting, spelling, punctuation, grammar, and capitalization. These tools are all important to writing fluency.

HANDWRITING

Sensory Letters, Slate Writing, and Say It As You Write It, from the previous section, can all be used to develop handwriting skills.

Copy It. For handwriting practice, have students copy words, poetry, or a short piece of writing. Students should be given ample practice in this way so that letter formation becomes automatic. Many commercial handwriting programs include this type of practice, but I recommend having students copy more meaningful pieces, such as thank-you letters, chants they are reading, or daily class messages.

SPELLING

Dictate It. Having students write down sentences you've dictated is an excellent way to increase writing fluency and practice spelling patterns, punctuation, and capitalization. Develop sentences for students to write; they might include words with spelling patterns you're studying or vocabulary words. In the primary grades, begin with three-word sentences and gradually over time increase their length to up to ten words. Read the sentence aloud. Then repeat it slowly, pausing after phrases so the students can write the words down. Say it again as students check their written work. When students finish, have them take out a colored marker to correct their own papers as you write the sentence on the board. Immediate feedback promotes the learning of the mechanics.

Individual Spelling Lists. Use student writing to create individual spelling lists of words students need to practice. Regularly review the words, such as at the start of a guided reading session. Having a spelling list for each child can be an ongoing activity.

Spelling Vocabulary Words. When introducing vocabulary words for a reading selection, consider using them as spelling words. After you introduce the words for meaning, you can ask students to brainstorm other words that follow the same spelling pattern and write them down. For example, if the vocabulary word is *thought*, you can have the child use that vocabulary word to spell on the board the words *bought* and *brought*. This activity helps students understand that if they are having difficulty spelling a word, sometimes thinking of other known words that rhyme with it can be useful. They are developing their knowledge of spelling patterns.

Word Sorting. Create word cards for words generated in the activity above (vocabulary words and other words in their word family). Distribute the word cards and ask students to sort them by word family or spelling pattern; then discuss.

Look in the Book. Students should be held accountable for the spelling of words in their guided reading books, but only if they have the book available as they are writing. Using the book to help them spell as they write teaches students the strategy of using what they have around them to spell unfamiliar words

Punctuation

Dictate It. This activity, on p. 191, is also useful for teaching punctuation.

Place the Punctuation. Put the punctuation marks being studied on index cards. Then write sentences (from a book or sentences you create) on a sentence strip without punctuation. Give each student a card and have them put the correct punctuation mark at the appropriate place. Alternatively, you can have students write in the necessary punctuation.

Conferring. Individual conferring with students during writing time can be used to identify where punctuation belongs or to correct the placement of punctuation in the student's writing.

Capitalization

In addition to mini-lessons on specific rules and Dictate It (p. 191), conferring with individual students helps them learn to use proper capitalization.

Grammar

Individual conferring with students during writing time can be used to refine students' use of grammar in writing.

Noun-Verb Match-Up. Help students develop an awareness of subject and predicate with this fun activity. Select nouns and verbs (from stories being read, vocabulary lists, or content subjects) and write them on index cards. Give each student a noun and verb and have everyone write a complete sentence using the noun and verb. Have students read their sentences aloud, and give them immediate feedback.

☑ Genre Writing Activities

In the primary grades, students need to learn the concepts of audience, purpose, and format. They should understand that a format of writing is chosen to match why it is being written and for whom. If the purpose is to thank someone, a letter format is used; if the purpose is to inform, an essay format might be appropriate. The organization of the writing is important as well. Young children can be supported in writing down their ideas first and then making decisions as to the order of the ideas. A great deal of modeling is necessary to help students learn these basics of writing. In addition, the activities below help students develop as writers.

Rewriting Game. Select a reading selection that is an example of the writing form you want to teach, such as problem/resolution. Read the text aloud and then ask students to rewrite it using different characters and events, but keeping the same theme. This rewriting works best with short, repetitive, rhyming books. This activity helps familiarize students with the conventions of a particular genre.

Genre Organizers. Create graphic organizers that have spaces for the different components of a particular genre. For example, if the writing form is a problem/ resolution story, the organizer should have spaces for the characters, setting, problem, resolution, beginning, middle, and end. Students can use the organizer as an outline, and they can fill them in as a prewriting activity or in response to reading a story.

Interact with Writing. Interactive writing (Pinnell & McCarrier, 1993) is a useful tool in writing. You direct the writing and support students as they help you. Explain to children what is going to be written, to whom, and why (format, audience, purpose). Ask students what they know about this kind of writing. Then begin the writing, asking students what to say and how to say it, and inviting them up to write letters and words, as appropriate. Build upon what children know and supply any lacking knowledge. This interactive writing activity encourages risk-taking in writing and demonstrates the writing process.

STORY WRITING

Another aspect of writing in the primary grades is story writing. Story writing is creative and utilizes the students' own experiences with literature and life. Children especially enjoy this type of writing. In guided reading, it often takes the form of writing a story like the one that was just read or changing the story that was just read.

To write stories, students need to understand basic story elements and the framework of beginning, middle, and end. The story elements of title, author, illustrator, setting, characters, plot, and climax are appropriate for primary students.

What's Missing? Understanding beginning, middle, and end can be difficult for primary students. One activity to develop this concept is to present a story that has a part missing; you can make up your own story or delete a part from a storybook. Students identify the missing part and then, with your help, write in the part. Eventually, the students can write in the part independently.

Happy Endings. Give students the beginning and middle of a story and have them write the ending.

Story Starters. Story starters are helpful in motivating students to write stories. Give students a picture, introduction, or question to jumpstart their writing.

Story Organizers. Present a literary elements chart to the students. They fill in the details of the chart as a way of planning for their own writing. They use these charts to write a story.

Picture Stories. Encourage kindergarteners or beginning writers to use pictures to tell stories. This strategy helps pre-writers understand story sense and structure. Then students can dictate sentences or use inventive spelling to write about the pictures.

☑ Response Writing Activities

Responding to reading is a real-life writing skill that we can introduce in the primary grades by asking questions about our reading and discussing how to answer the questions. Basically, instruction emphasizes understanding what a question is and how to answer it. You can model using question stems in your responses and providing details from the text to support your answers. Finding appropriate details is another aspect of reading response.

Another type of response writing is called literature journal response. This response writing involves teaching children how to be active readers and how to respond to their reading in journals. This type of response writing is more often done in the upper grades. However, Wollman-Bonilla and Werchadlo (1999) discuss a study of first graders and the use of this type of response writing. They found that teacher scaffolding of instruction and analysis of the responses promoted journal writing in first graders. The responses were categorized into two kinds: text-centered and reader-centered. Analyzing the responses provided the teachers with direction for their instruction.

Oral Practice. Have students respond orally to questions about a text you've read together. Have them respond in complete sentences using the question stem to begin their answer. (For example, if the question is, "How did Max feel when Ruby put him in the bath the second time?" they could begin an answer with, "Max felt _____ when Ruby put him in the bath the second time.")

Question-and-Answer. Write questions about a text on index cards. Give each student a different question and have them write the answer in a complete sentence using the sentence stem. Students then read their question and answer to the group. The group analyzes the responses to see if they used the question stem and answered the question.

Journaling. Journal writing is a good activity for students who are writing fluently. As students read chapters or selections, have them write a journal entry about what they are reading. This entry could take the form of asking questions, making predictions about the story, making personal connections, connecting to another text, or putting oneself in the story. Be sure to model the various types of entries before asking students to write.

☑ Enhancement Writing Activities

Introduce students who can write simple sentences to a variety of sentence structures and descriptors to foster their growth as writers.

Add-On. Present simple sentences, such as "I like" or "We ride." Ask students to build longer, more descriptive sentences by adding words. For example, *I like to run. I like to run fast. The little girls and I like to run fast.* Talk about how each word changes the meaning of the sentence.

A Picture Is Worth a Thousand Words. Select a detailed picture of an object and ask students to list as many words as possible to describe the object. Contribute rich, descriptive words to develop students' vocabularies. Write the words on a chart, saving them for later reference.

In summary, writing is an important ability to develop in the primary grades. In guided reading instruction, teachers have the opportunity to teach several different aspects of writing. One of the most important understandings of writing instruction is the integration of reading and writing. Helping students become successful writers is one of our goals for literacy development.

☑ Parent Home Activities for Writing

Handwriting Practice Activity. Many times K–2 students have sloppy handwriting or form letters incorrectly. Sometimes children take an exceptionally long time to write a word. This activity will help your child to improve handwriting accuracy and speed.

Find or write a simple sentence for your child to copy. If he/she has trouble with writing letters or words, select a few letters or words for him/her to copy. With the printed sentence, letters, or words next to your child, have him/her quickly copy it. Only allow 20 seconds for copying, then count the number of letters formed correctly. Give your child another sentence to copy. Time the practice and then calculate the number of letters correctly copied. Let your child work toward beating the previous score. Keep each session brief so it does not become tiresome.

Read Aloud/Writing Activity. After reading a book to your child, ask him/her to respond to some comprehension questions (see Parent Comprehension Activities, page 178) in writing. You will need to support and guide your child by helping him/her with words, spelling, and punctuation. It is best to keep the activity focused on a couple of questions so your child doesn't spend a long time on the activity and become tired. This activity works best with first and second graders.

Writing a Story Together Activity. This activity requires some paper and pencils for you and your child. Together, decide on a topic or story to write about. If you are writing about a topic, then have the child come up with some facts about it. If you're writing a story, decide on the beginning, middle, and end. Next, write one sentence while your child observes. Then have your child write a sentence, guiding him/her by spelling words or putting in punctuation, if necessary. Take turns writing sentences in this manner, and your child can illustrate if he/she would like. Then your child can practice reading the story aloud.

Different Ending to Read Aloud Story. After you have read a story to your child, discuss how the ending could have been different. Together write a different ending to the story. You can guide your child's writing by supplying words, spelling words, or putting in the punctuation, if necessary. Your child can illustrate this different ending.

Dictate It. This activity can help reluctant writers develop their ability to write. Whatever the writing task is, ask your child to dictate what he/she would like to say, and write it down. You can have your child help you decide what punctuation is necessary, where it goes, or where the capital letters go. Then have your child read the sentences to you a couple of times to become fluent with them. It is best to start with one or a couple of sentences first and then increase the number of sentences.

Spelling Practice Activity. Ask your child's teacher for a spelling word list appropriate for your child's grade level. Here is one way to practice these words:

• Write the letters in each word on small cards, then pull out the letters of the first word to be spelled. Scramble the letters and ask your child to put the letters in order to spell the word correctly, without looking at the word. Then have your child check his/her letter card order with the whole word. If there is an error, repeat the activity. The number of words to practice with can be determined by the motivation and enthusiasm of your child.

Final Thoughts

As I reflect on the content of this book, my hope is that it will enhance your knowledge of literacy development and what you can do to help all children be successful in learning to read and write. For 30 years I have been committed to the belief that all children can learn literacy, if given the appropriate instruction. I feel it is our responsibility to find the appropriate method or technique that will assist every child in learning literacy.

This book is my contribution to the quest of providing the opportunity for all students to reach their potential regardless of what experiences they bring to school. We need to give children the stories that will sustain them in life and the tools to express their own stories of life. I hope this book will provide you with more stepping stones in your literacy journey with children, our future in making this world a better place to live.

Appendix

How to Make the Mini-Books

Each mini-book page is half of an 8½ x 11 book page.

First, make copies of the page with the cover and the page with page 2. Make these pages into a double-sided cover sheet. (See illustration.) Fold this page so that the cover is face up. When you open it, the story will start on the left-hand side, on page 2.

Next, make one-sided copies of the interior pages. The first set is always pages 3 and 4. Fold each of these interior pages so the printed side faces out; keep the fold to the right. (See illustration.) Place them in order inside the cover page.

Finally, staple the mini-book together on the spine.

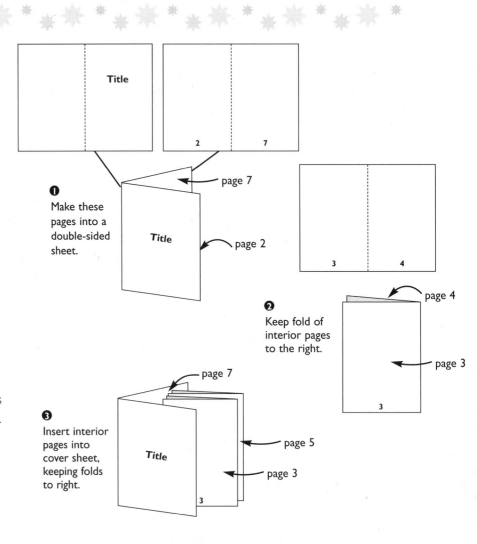

Class **R**ecord **S**heet _____

Teacher _____ Grade _____ Date _____

Assessment Items

Student										
....										
....										
....										
....										
....										
....										
....										
....										
....										
....										
....										
....										
....										
....										
....										
....										
....										
....										
....										
....										
....										
....										

Name _____ **Date** _____

Name _____ **Date** _____

Literary Elements Chart

Title _____

Author _____ Genre: Fiction or Nonfiction

Setting (where and when) _____

_____

Main character(s) _____

Other characters _____

_____

Plot events _____

_____

_____

_____

_____

_____

Climax _____

_____

Problem _____

_____

Resolution _____

Letter Recognition Scoring Sheet

Name _____　Date _____

Directions: Ask child to point to each letter and say its name. Upper- or lowercase does not have to be said with letter to be correct. Circle the letters child reads incorrectly.

Criterion for Kindergarten B Assessment: 40/52
Criterion for Kindergarten C Assessment: 50/52

Order of Presentation:

C	f	O	P	t	c
D	F	o	T	p	R
I	S	m	j	A	d
M	n	a	B	I	u
b	N	E	G	r	Q
i	s	g	H	e	h
q	Z	Y	w	J	K
v	z	X	W	k	L
U	V	x	y		

Letter Recognition Presentation Sheet

C	f	O	P	t	c
D	F	o	T	p	R
I	S	m	j	A	d
M	n	a	B	I	u
b	N	E	G	r	Q
i	s	g	H	e	h
q	Z	Y	w	J	K
v	z	X	W	k	L
U	V	x	y		

Writing the **A**lphabet

Name _____ Date _____

Directions: Explain to children that they will be writing the upper- and lowercase letters of each letter you say. For example, you might say "Write the uppercase and lowercase c in this box" as you point to the first box. If children cannot write a letter, tell them to leave the box blank and try to write the next letter in the next box.

Scoring: Each letter, such as P and p, counts as one point. Reversals are counted as correct unless they produce another letter, such as b for d.

Order of Presentation:

Cc	Oo	Ff	Pp	Tt
Dd	Rr	Ss	Mm	Aa
Jj	Nn	Bb	Ii	Uu
Ee	Gg	Qq	Hh	Zz
Yy	Ww	Kk	Ll	Xx
Vv				

Writing the **A**lphabet

Name _____   Date _____

I Like Fruit

by Brenda M. Weaver

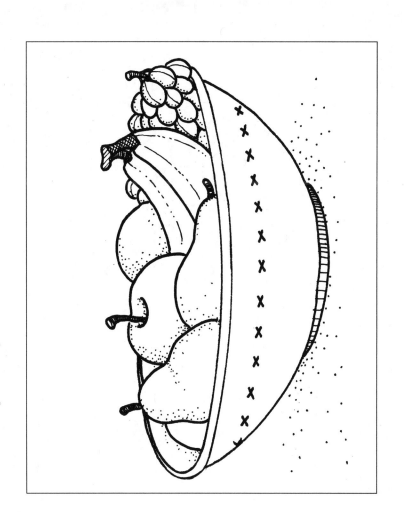

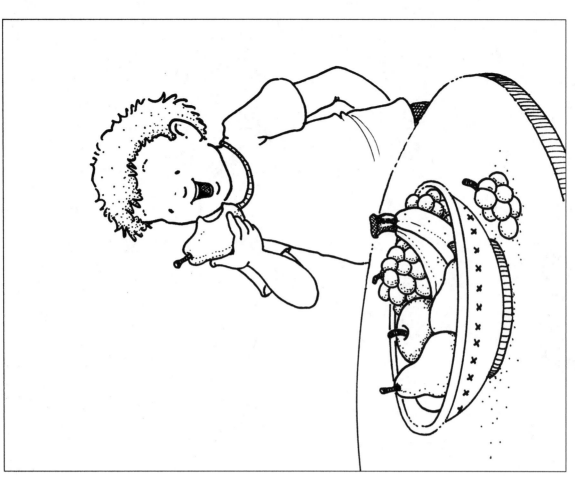

I like fruit.

I like apples.

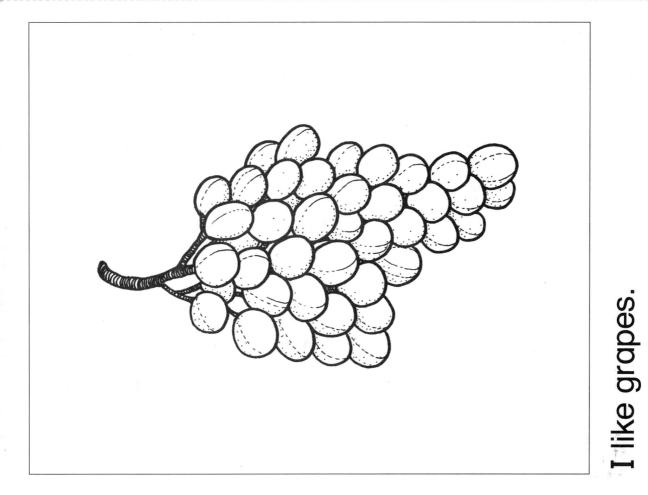

I like bananas.

I like grapes.

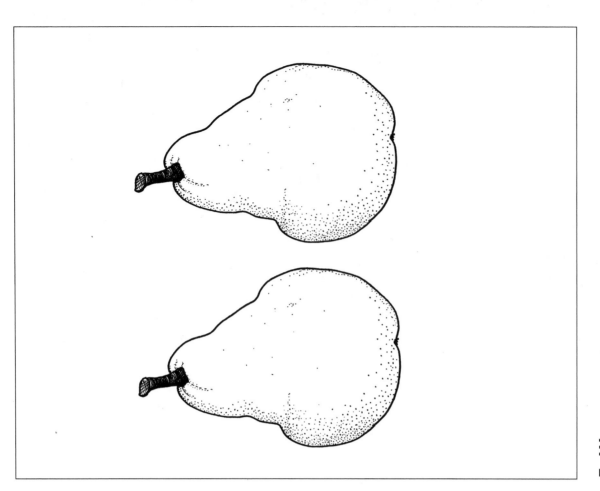

I like pears.

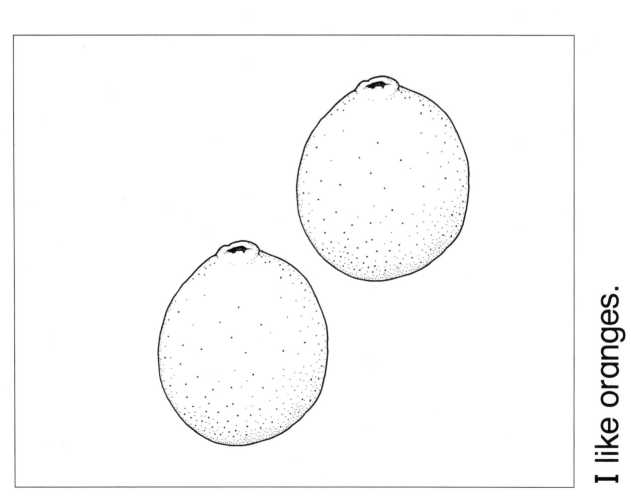

I like oranges.

I Like to Eat Food

by Brenda M. Weaver

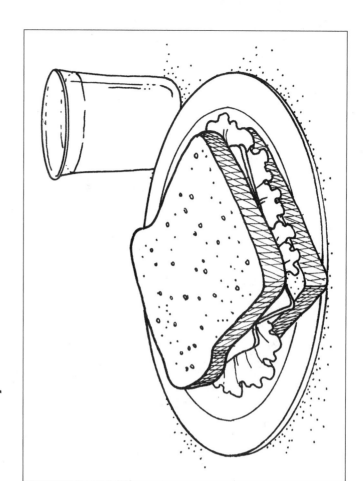

I like to eat food.

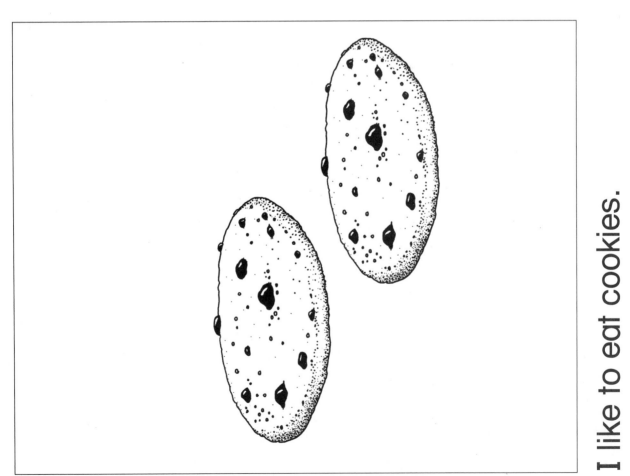

I like to eat cookies.

I like to eat bananas.

4

I like to eat sandwiches.

3

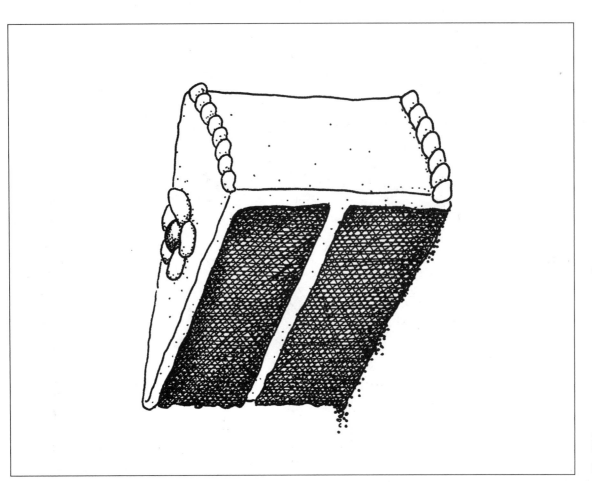

I like to eat cake.

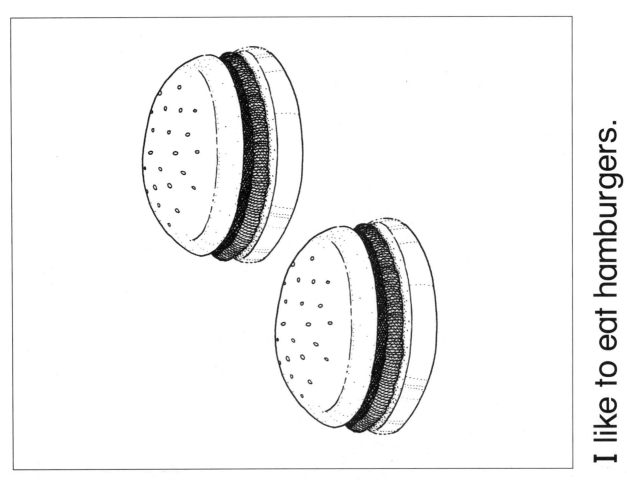

I like to eat hamburgers.

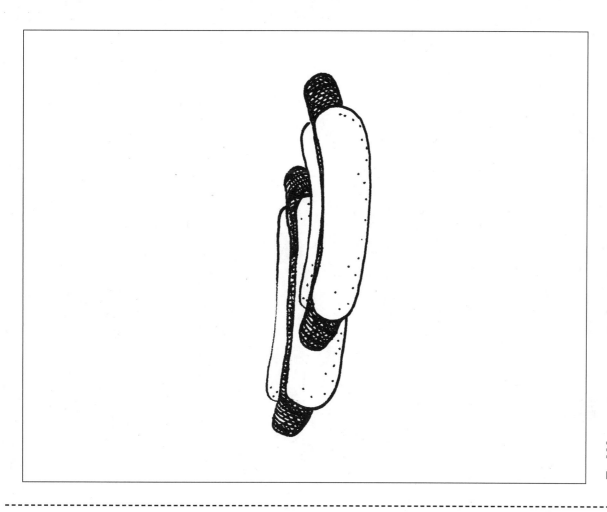

I like to eat hot dogs.

8

I like to eat pizza.

7

At the Zoo

by Brenda M. Weaver

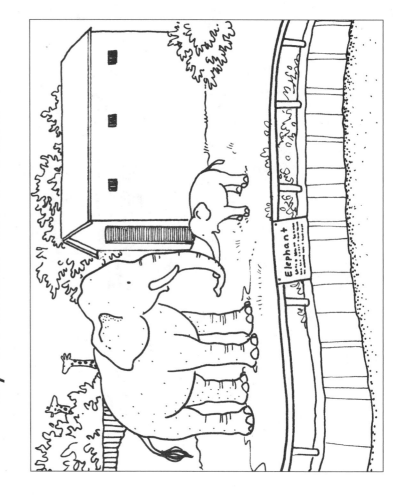

All are at the zoo.

9

There are elephants.

2

There are monkeys.

There are zebras.

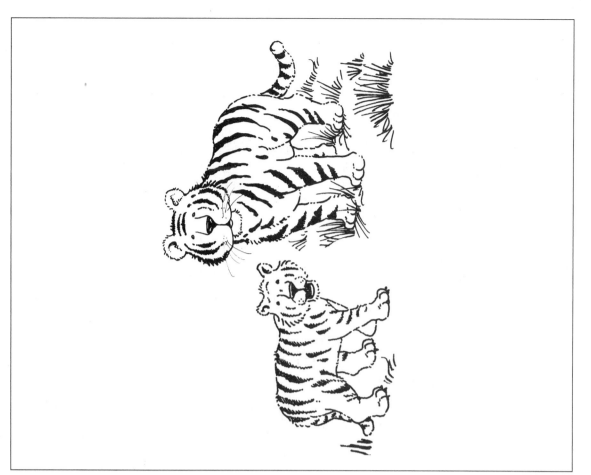

There are tigers.

There are snakes.

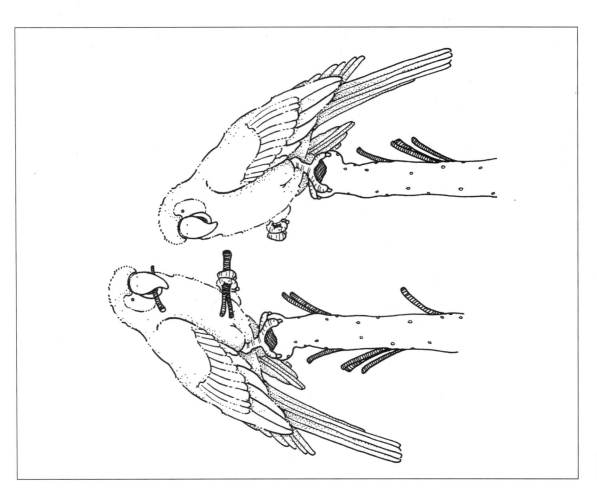

There are parrots.

There are lions.

Fish

by Brenda M. Weaver

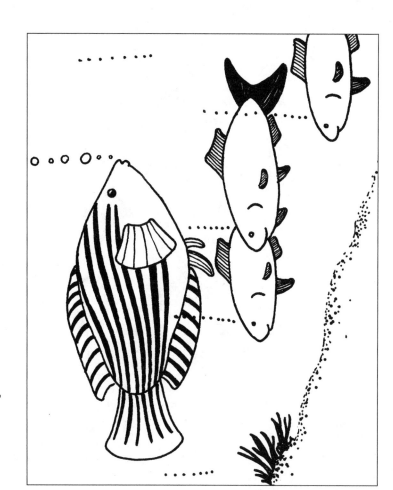

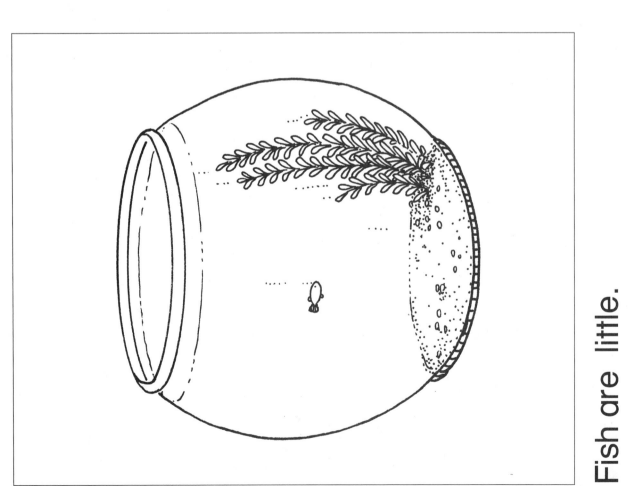

What do fish do?

Fish are little.

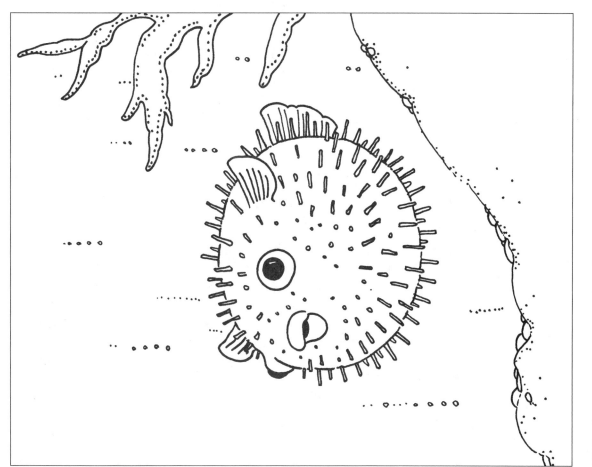

Fish are round.

4

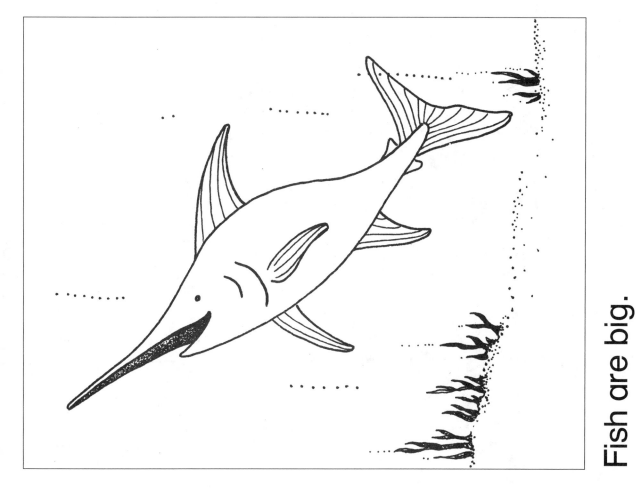

Fish are big.

3

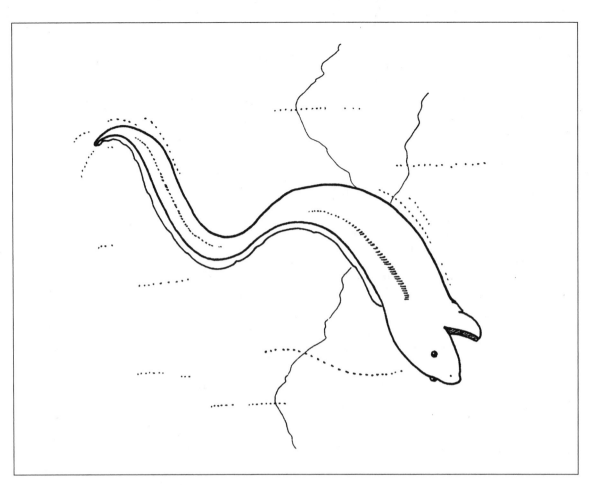

Fish are long.

Fish are spotted.

Fish are scary.

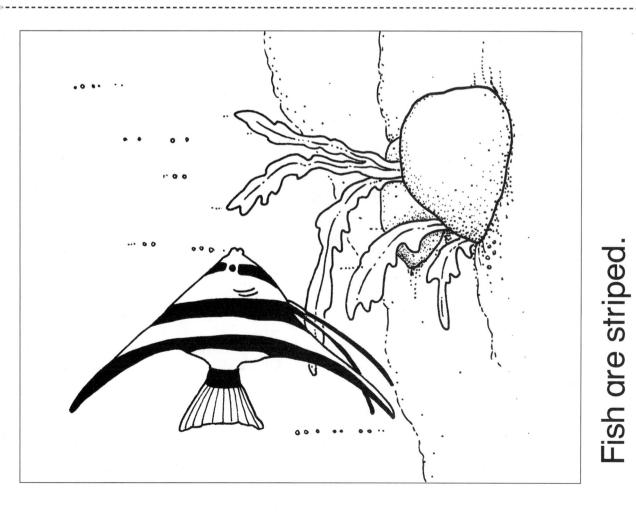

Fish are striped.

Little Bug, Little Bug

by Brenda M. Weaver

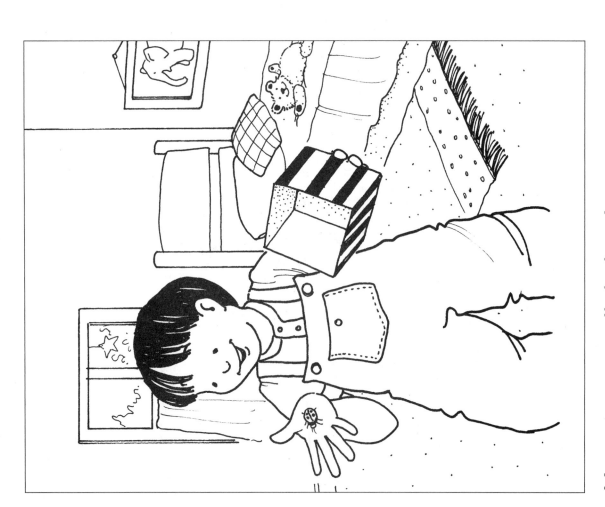

Here you are, little bug!

Are you in the box?

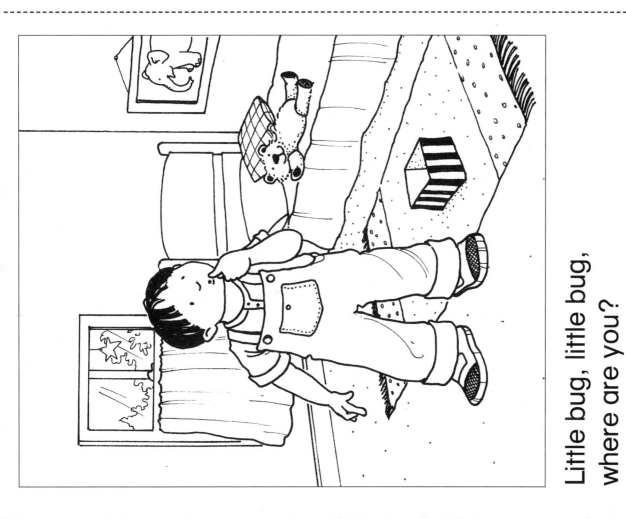

Little bug, little bug,
where are you?

Little bug, little bug,
where are you?

Are you under the bed?

Little bug, little bug,
where are you?

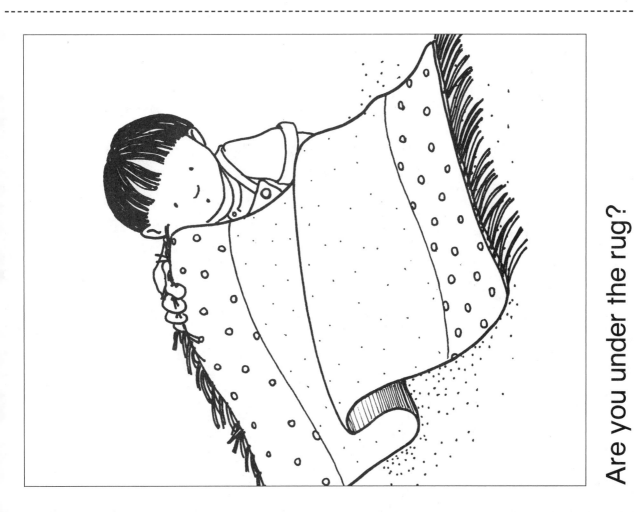

Are you under the rug?

My Cat
Is Lost

by Brenda M. Weaver

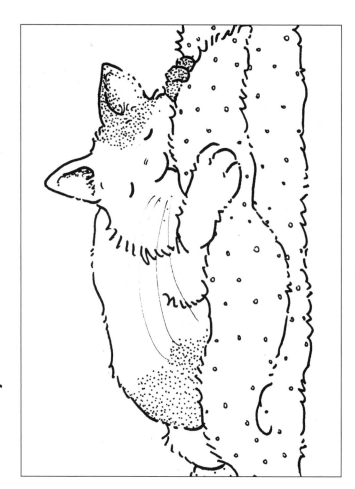

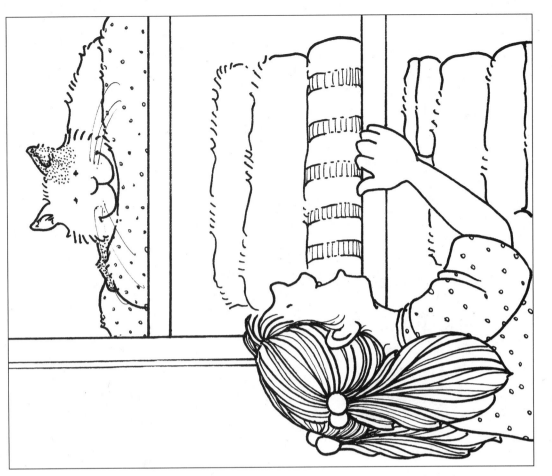

There's Buffy sleeping on
the blanket.

Buffy is my cat.

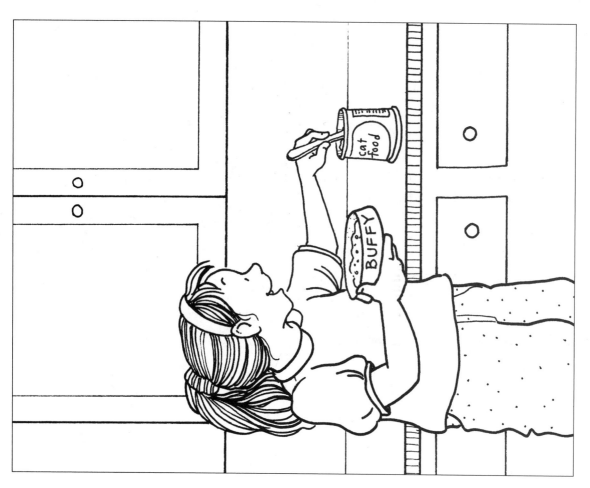

I feed Buffy.

We play with a ball.

I look in the kitchen. No Buffy.

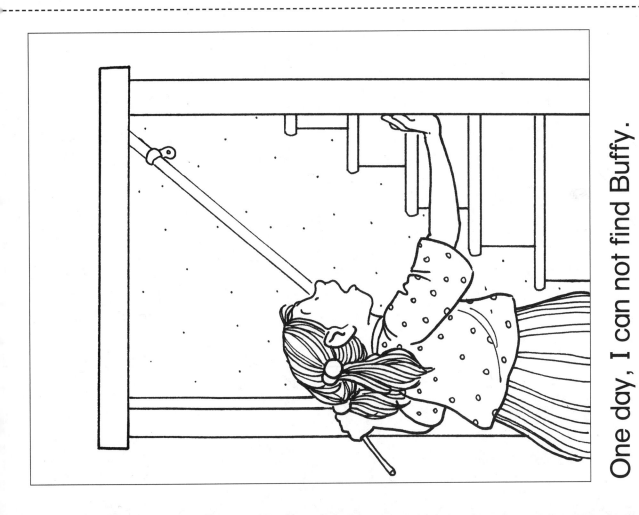

One day, I can not find Buffy.

I look in the closet.

I look my bedroom. No Buffy.

Frisco and Pippin Are Friends

by Brenda M. Weaver

Frisco and Pippin lie in the sun to dry off.
Frisco and Pippin are great friends!

12

When the dogs get tired, they jump out and shake the water off. The girls still play in the pool.

Frisco is a gray dog. He lives with Alicia.

One day Frisco sees Pippin playing next door.

Pippin is a brown and white dog. She lives with Kayla. Alicia and Kayla are friends.

Kayla calls, "Pippin, come. It's time for dinner." Alicia calls, "Frisco, come. Here's your food." Both dogs keep playing.

6

Frisco runs over to Pippin. They sniff noses and wag their tails. Then they begin to chase each other. They are having fun.

5

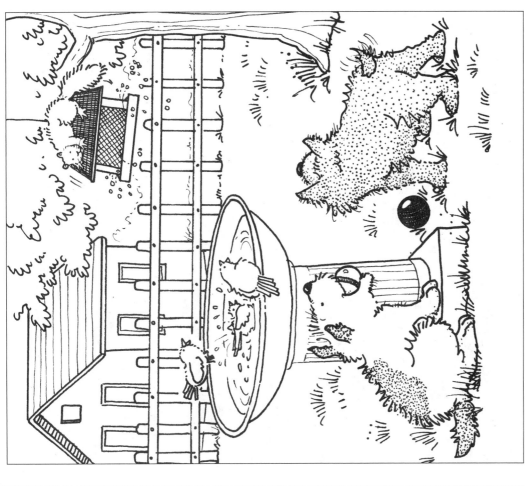

After eating, Pippin and Frisco play together in Pippin's yard. They see a squirrel on the bird feeder.

8

Kayla runs to get Pippin. Alicia runs to get Frisco. Both dogs go home for dinner.

7

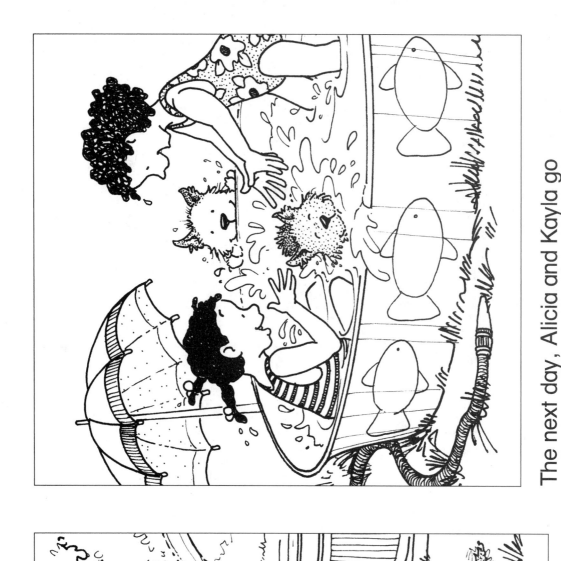

The next day, Alicia and Kayla go
swimming. Pippin and Frisco go with them.
The dogs jump in the pool.
They splash and swim with the girls.

The dogs run to the tree and bark at the
squirrel. They bark until Alicia and Kayla call
them.

The Mystery of the Missing Cat Food

Betsy Franco

Joe and I gave each other a thumbs up. We had solved the mystery of the missing cat food!

12

In came Rap, wagging his tail. "He's been getting a bit chubby lately, hasn't he?" said Mr. Green.

11

It all started the morning that Snowflake's cat food was missing from her bowl.

2

"It must be a mouse," my brother Joe said.

"But a little mouse just couldn't eat that much food," I said.

"It must be something bigger."

3

"Let's put out flour all over the kitchen floor. That way we can get some footprints to study," I said.

4

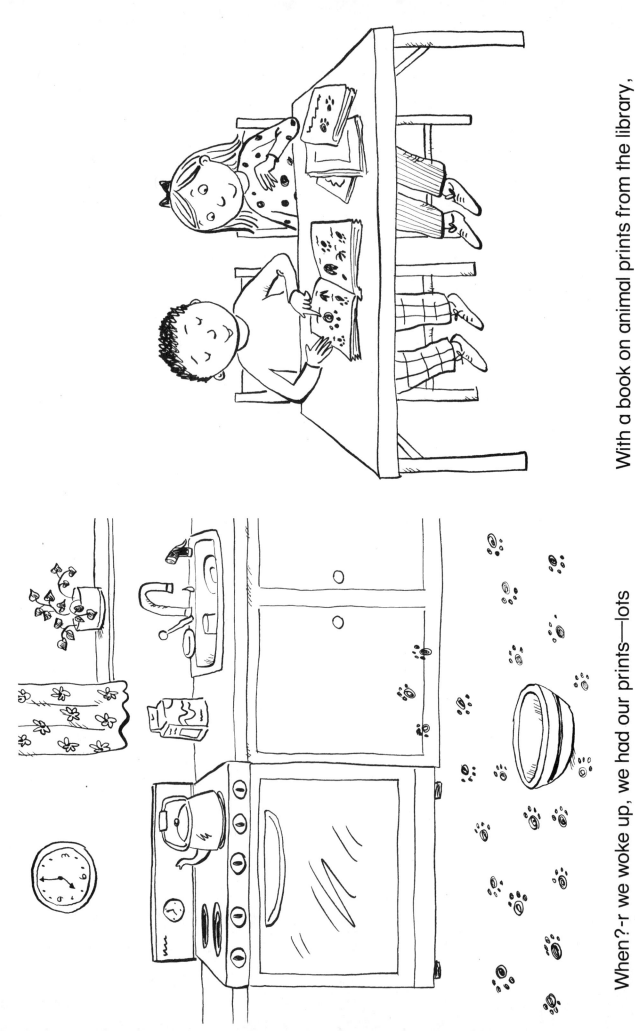

With a book on animal prints from the library, we narrowed it down to a dog.

6

When?-r we woke up, we had our prints—lots u736of them.

5

Joe and I made a list of the dogs in the neighborhood. The only small dogs we knew were Shadow and Rap.

Next, we had to figure out how big a dog. "That dog is getting through the cat door so it must be as small as a cat," said Joe.

Next, we went to see Rap's owner.
"At night, I just let Rap out for a short run in the dark. He always comes right back," said Mr. Green.

First we went to see Mrs. Brown, the lady down the street. She owned Shadow.

"We never let Shadow out without a leash," she said. "It couldn't be Shadow."

Lost in the Snow

by Betsy Franco

"You took a wrong turn. But I can see you used your heads. I'm very proud of you," said their dad. "And I sure am glad we found you!"

12

Jack and Jessica crawled quickly out of the snow cave.

"Dad!" they shouted as they ran to their father.

They all hugged tightly together.

The twins, Jack and Jessica, loved to ski. They were even better than their dad. In fact, they were way ahead of him on the ski slope.

"We must have taken a wrong turn off the path," said Jessica.

"Hello, hello, does anyone hear us?" they yelled.

But no one yelled back.

4

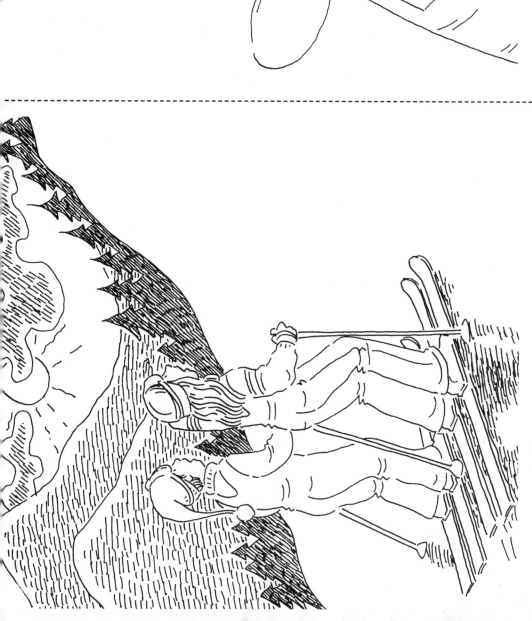

"Let's stop and wait for Dad," said Jack. It was the last run of the day. They waited and waited but they couldn't find Dad. In fact, they couldn't see anyone at all.

3

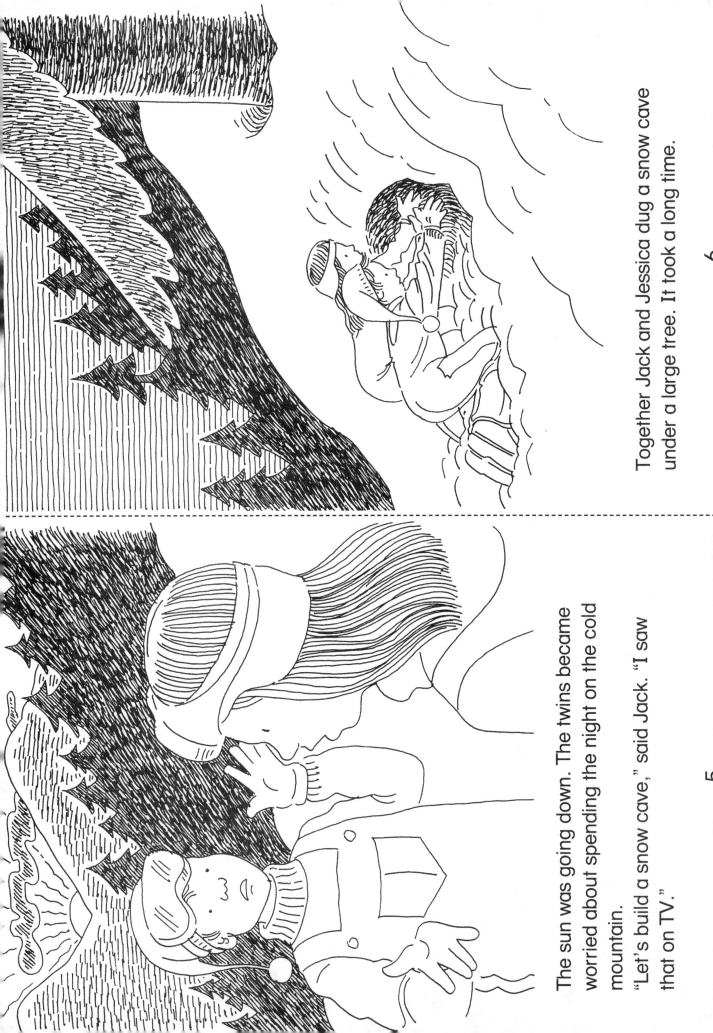

Together Jack and Jessica dug a snow cave under a large tree. It took a long time.

6

The sun was going down. The twins became worried about spending the night on the cold mountain.

"Let's build a snow cave," said Jack. "I saw that on TV."

5

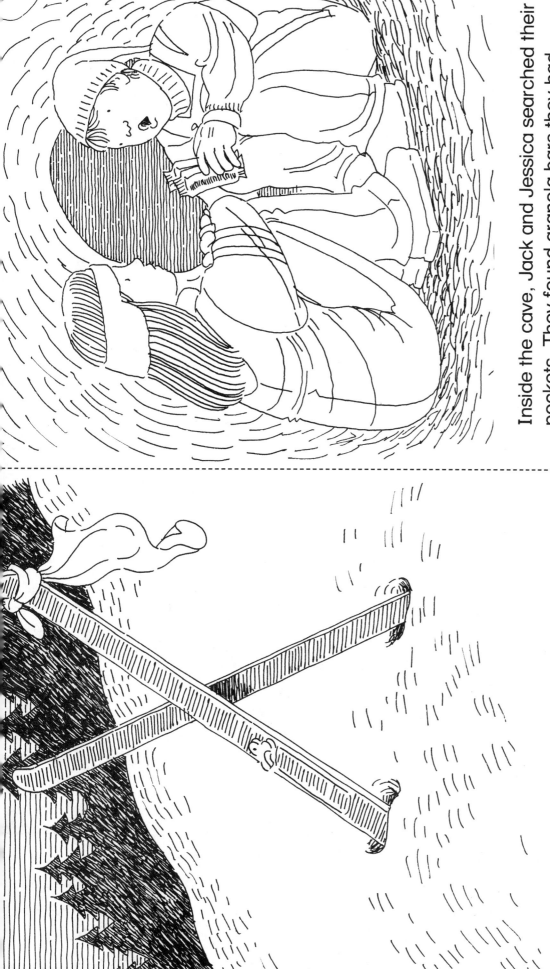

They put their skis in an X shape and placed
Jessica's red scarf around the top of it.
"That way, someone might spot us," said Jessica.

7

Inside the cave, Jack and Jessica searched their
pockets. They found granola bars they had
packed for a snack.
"We'll have to eat this food a little at a time,"
said Jack.

8

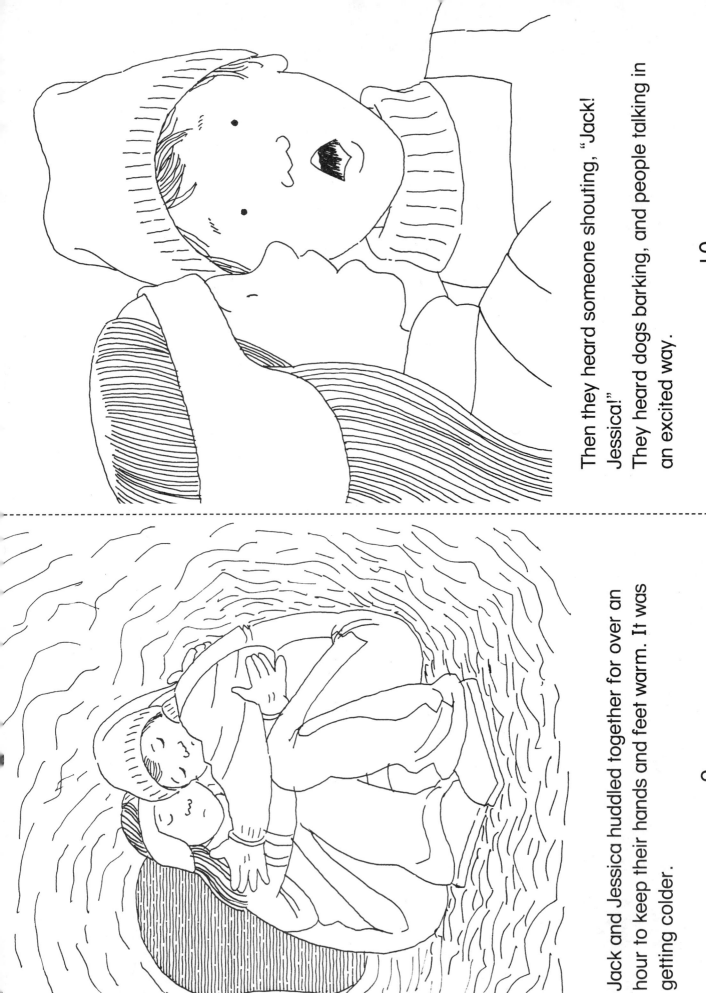

Then they heard someone shouting, "Jack! Jessica!"
They heard dogs barking, and people talking in an excited way.

10

Jack and Jessica huddled together for over an hour to keep their hands and feet warm. It was getting colder.

9

Jane Goodall and the Chimps

by Betsy Franco

1

Whenever she can, Jane returns to Africa to be with the chimps. She also writes books and gives talks. She wants to help people understand why it is so important to take care of wild animals and the habitats in which they live.

12

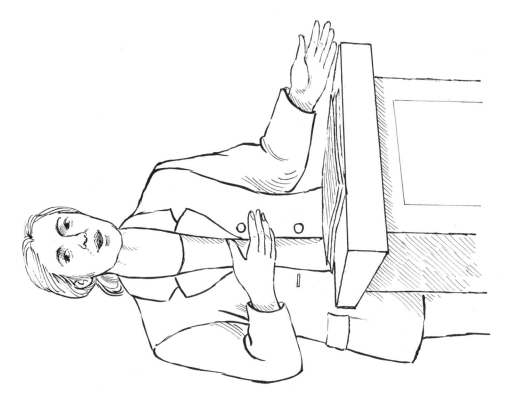

Jane soon became famous and was asked to speak to people all around the world. No one had ever watched wild chimps and learned so much about them. Jane's knowledge helped scientists understand human beings better.

11

From the time she was very young, Jane Goodall loved to watch birds and animals near her home in England. Her favorite toy was a stuffed chimpanzee named Jubilee.

2

Jane always wanted to go to Africa where there were lots of wild animals. Then, when she was older, a friend who lived in Africa invited Jane for a visit. Jane worked hard to save money for the trip.

4

When Jane was four years old, she sat for hours in the hen house. Later, she told her mother that she had waited and waited there to watch a hen lay an egg.

3

Dr. Leakey invited Jane to study a group of chimpanzees in Africa. She was thrilled to live with the chimps and study them. She invited her mother to come with her.

6

In Africa, Jane met a famous scientist named Dr. Louis Leakey. She helped him dig up bones that had been buried for millions of years.

5

Finally, after many months, she saw a group of chimps. From then on she watched them quietly for hours every day. Sometimes she slept near them. Eventually, Jane gave the chimps names like Flo, Fifi, and Mr. McGregor.

8

Jane and her mother lived alone in two small tents in the middle of the jungle. Every day Jane would go looking for chimps.

7

Jane studied how families and groups of chimps got along. She discovered how smart they are when she saw a chimp make a tool. The chimp took the leaves off of a stick. Then it poked the stick in a termite hole and pulled up termites to eat.

After five months, the chimps had at last grown used to Jane. David Graybeard was the name of the first chimp to touch her. She held a nut in her hand. He reached for it and held her hand softly.

Parent Book Selection and Reading Chart

The following information may help to select an appropriate book for your child and explains different ways you can read to or with your child.

Definition of Terms Used in Chart

1. **Child interaction with adult sharing:** Adult reads book and child repeats phrases or joins in on rhymes, etc.
2. **Adult sharing:** Adult reads book to child and child listens or asks questions. Child may make minor interactions.
3. **Child interaction and reading:** Child selects book and reads independently. At younger ages, child may paraphrase reading of text.

Age/ Grade Level	Characteristics of Books for Child Interaction With Adult Sharing	Characteristics of Books for Adult Sharing	Characteristics of Books for Child Interaction and Reading
Kindergarten	Picture books with simple concepts, simple plots, rhyming, rhythm, repetition, and pictures supporting text Exemplar Book: *Guess How Much I Love You* by Sam McBratney	Picture books with simple story lines or simple informational text Exemplar Book: *Bumpety Bump* by Pat Hutchins	Wordless books, one-word books (naming), one sentence per page with repetitive text supported by pictures Exemplar Book: *Where's Spot?* by Eric Hill
Beginning Grade 1	Picture books with simple story lines or simple informational text Exemplar Books: *Don't Forget the Bacon!* by Pat Hutchins; *The Cat in the Hat* by Dr. Seuss	Picture books with story lines that have some interpretation or humor or/and informational text with some descriptive detail Exemplar Books: *The Very Quiet Cricket* by Eric Carle; *Curious George at the Baseball Game* by H. A. Rey	One or two sentences per page with repetitive or predictable text supported by pictures Exemplar Book: *The Napping House* by Audrey and Don Wood
Second Half of Grade 1	Picture books with simple story lines or simple informational text or "I Can Read" type chapter books Exemplar Books: *Little Bear*; *Frog and Toad Are Friends* by Arnold Lobel	Picture books with story lines that have some interpretation or humor or/and informational text with some descriptive detail; short, simple chapter books Exemplar Book: *Koala Lou* by Mem Fox	Text can be half to full page; words are high-frequency words or rhyming; text is somewhat supported by pictures Exemplar Book: *Lunch Box Surprise* by Grace Maccarone
Beginning Grade 2	Simple chapter books or informational text with descriptive details Exemplar Book: *Junie B.* books by B. Park	Chapter books and more complex informational text Exemplar Book: *Catwings* by Ursula LeGuin	Text can be full page with high-frequency words, simple sentences but several pages long (up to 20 pages) Exemplar Books: *Annie's Pet* by Barbara Brenner; *As I Was Crossing the Boston Common* by Norma Farber
Second Half of Grade 2	Simple chapter books or informational text with descriptive details Exemplar Books: *Henry & Mudge* books by Cynthia Rylant	Chapter books and more complex informational text Exemplar Books: *Freckle Juice* by Judy Blume; *All About Sharks* by Jim Arnosky	Text is full page with high-frequency words, simple compound sentences and several pages long (up to 30 pages); simple chapter books Exemplar Books: *Frog & Toad* series by Arnold Lobel; *Keep the Lights Burning Abbie* by Peter Roop

Bibliography

Adams, M. J. (1990). *Beginning to read: Thinking and learning about print.* Cambridge, MA: MIT Press.

Allington, R. L. (2001). *What really matters for struggling readers: Designing research-based programs.* New York: Addison-Wesley Educational Publishers.

Anderson, R. C. & Pearson, P. D. (1984). A schema-theoretic view of basic processes in reading. In P. D. Pearson (Ed.), *Handbook of reading research* (pp. 255–292). White Plains, NY: Longman.

Beck, I. L., & McKeown, M. G. (2001). Text talk: Capturing the benefits of read-aloud experiences for young children. *Reading Teacher,* 55 (1), 10–20.

Clay, M. M. (1993a). *An observation survey of early literacy achievement.* Portsmouth, NH: Heinemann.

Clay, M. M. (1993b). *Reading recovery: A guidebook for teachers in training.* Portsmouth, NH: Heinemann.

Clay, M. M. (1991). *Becoming literate: The construction of inner control.* Portsmouth, NH: Heinemann.

Cooper, J. D. (1993). *Literacy: Helping children construct meaning.* Boston: Houghton Mifflin.

DeLorenzo, J. P. (April 2008). *Letter to Superintendents.* Albany, NY.

Dowhower, S. L. (1999). Supporting a strategic stance in the classroom: A comprehension framework for helping teachers help students to be strategic. *Reading Teacher,* 52 (7), 672–688.

Ehri, L. C. (1994). Development of the ability to read words: Update. In R. B. Ruddell, M. R. Ruddell, & H. Singer (Eds.), *Theoretical models and processes of reading* (pp. 323–358). Newark, DE: International Reading Association.

Fountas, I. C., & Pinnell, G. S. (1996). *Guided reading: Good first teaching for all children.* Portsmouth, NH: Heinemann.

Gardner, H. (1983). *Frames of mind: The theory of multiple intelligences.* New York, NY: Basic Books.

Gardner, H. (1993). *Multiple intelligences: The theory in practice.* New York: Basic Books.

Gentry, J. R. (1984). Developmental aspects of learning to spell. *Academic Therapy,* 20, 11–19.

Graves, D. H. (1994). *A fresh look at writing.* Portsmouth, NH: Heinemann.

Graves, D. H. (1983). *Writing: Teachers and children at work.* Portsmouth, NH: Heinemann.

Harris, T. L. & Hodges, R. E. (Eds.). (1995). *The literacy dictionary.* Newark, DE: International Reading Association.

Harvey, S., & Goudvis, A. (2000). *Strategies that work.* Portland, ME: Stenhouse Publishers.

Individuals With Disabilities Education Improvement Act (IDEA) of 2004, PL 108-446, 20 U.S. C. §§ 1400 et seq.

Johnston, F. (1998). The reader, the text, and the task: Learning words in first grade. *Reading Teacher,* 51 (8), 666–675.

Johnston, F. (2001). The utility of phonic generalizations: Let's take another look at Clymer's conclusions. *Reading Teacher,* 55 (2), 132–143.

Keene, E. O., & Zimmermann, S. (1997). *Mosaic of thought.* Portsmouth, NH: Heinemann.

McLaughlin, M. (2003). *Guided comprehension in the primary grades.* Newark, DE: International Reading Association.

Miller, B., & Giugno, M. (September, 2008). *Implications of RTI implementation for NYS schools presentation.* New York State Education Department.

Mooney, M. E. (1990). *Reading to, with, and by children.* Katonah, NY: Richard C. Owen Publishers.

Moustafa, M., & Maldonado-Colon, E. (1999). Whole-to-parts phonics instruction: Building on what children know to help them know more. *Reading Teacher,* 52 (5), 448–458.

Murray, B. A., & Lesniak, T. (1999). The letterbox lesson: A hands-on approach for teaching decoding. *Reading Teacher,* 52 (6), 644–650.

National Joint Committee on Learning Disabilities. (2005). *Responsiveness to intervention and learning disabilities.* LD online: www.ldonline.org.

Oster, L. (2001).Using the think-aloud for reading instruction. *Reading Teacher,* 55 (1), 64–69.

Pearson, P. D., & Stephens, D. (1994). Learning about literacy: A 30-year journey. In R. B. Ruddell, M. R. Ruddell, & H. Singer (Eds.), *Theoretical models and processes of reading* (pp. 22–42). Newark, DE: International Reading Association.

Pearson, P. D., Roehler, L. R., Dole, J. A., & Duffy, G. (1992). Developing expertise in reading comprehension. In S. J. Samuels, & A. E. Farstrup (Eds.). *What research has to say about reading instruction* (pp. 145–199). Newark, DE: International Reading Association.

Perfetti, C. A. (1985). *Reading ability.* New York: Oxford University Press.

Pinnell, G. S., & McCarrier, A. (1993). Interactive writing: A transition tool for assisting children in learning to read and write. In E. Hiebert & B. Taylor (Eds.). *Getting reading right from the start: Effective early literacy interventions* (pp.149–170). Needham Heights, MA: Allyn & Bacon.

Portalupi, J. (2000). Learning to write: Honoring both process and product. *Trends and issues in elementary language arts,* 2000 Edition (pp. 27–34). Urbana, IL: National Council of Teachers of English.

Samuels, S. J., Schermer, N., & Reinking, D. (1992). Reading fluency: Techniques for making decoding automatic. In S. J. Samuels, & A. E. Farstrup (Eds.). *What research has to say about reading instruction* (pp. 124–144). Newark, DE: International Reading Association.

Schulman, M. B. & Payne, C. D. (2000). *Guided reading: Making it work.* New York: Scholastic.

Shanahan, T. (2008). Implications of RTI for the reading teacher. In D. Fuchs, L. Fuchs, and S. Vaughn (Eds.), *Response to intervention: A framework for reading educators*. Newark, DE: International Reading Association.

Stahl, S. A., & Kuhn, M. R. (2002). Making it sound like language: Developing fluency. *Reading Teacher*, 55 (6), 582–584.

The State Education Department/The University of the State of New York.

Taylor, B. M. (1992). Text structure, comprehension and recall. In S. J. Samuels & A. E. Farstrup, *What research has to say about reading instruction* (pp. 220–235). Newark, DE: International Reading Association.

Weaver, B. M. (2000). *Leveling books K–6: Matching readers to text*. Newark, DE: International Reading Association.

Williams, T. L., & Baumann, J. F. (2008). *Contemporary research on effective elementary literacy teachers*. 57th Yearbook of the National Reading Conference. Oak Creek, WI: National Reading Conference, Inc.

Winters, R. (2001). Vocabulary anchors: Building conceptual connections with young readers. *Reading Teacher*, 54 (7), 659–662.

Wolfe, P. (2001). *Brain matters: Translating research into classroom practice*. Alexandria, VA: Association for Supervision and Curriculum Development.

Wolfe, P., & Brandt, R. (1998). What do we know from brain research? *Educational Leadership*, 56 (3), 8–13.

Wollman-Bonilla, J. E., & Werchadlo, B. (1999). Teacher and peer roles in scaffolding first graders' responses to literature. *Reading Teacher*, 52 (6), 598–607.

Weaver Literacy Research Support

The Weaver Literacy components were developed based upon research in learning and language arts. Each element in the assessments was carefully created to assess the aspect of literacy acquisition deemed critical to literacy development supported by research. In addition to this research base, the components have been revised to ensure teacher-friendly and student-friendly accessibility. Furthermore, standardized test results and New York State Grade 4 English/Language Arts Test results verify the reliability of Weaver Literacy. The research studies are listed below the sections. For further information on Weaver Literacy visit the website: www.weaverliteracy.com

Model of Learning

Brandt, R. (1998). *Powerful learning*. Alexandria, VA: Association for Supervision and Curriculum Development.

Wolfe, P. (2001). *Brain matters: Translating research into classroom practice*. Alexandria, VA: Association for Supervision and Curriculum Development.

Word Recognition (cueing strategies, oral fluency, word study)

Clay, M. M. (1979). *Reading: The patterning of complex behavior*. Portsmouth, NH: Heinemann.

Mooney, M. (1988). *Developing life-long readers*. Wellington, New Zealand: Department of Education.

Clay, M. M. (1993a). *An observation survey of early literacy achievement*. Portsmouth, NH: Heinemann.

Clay, M. M. (1991). *Becoming literate: The construction of inner control*. Portsmouth, NH: Heinemann.

Clay, M. M. (1993b). *Reading recovery: A guidebook for teachers in training*. Portsmouth, NH: Heinemann.

Ehri, L. C. (1994). Development of the ability to read words: Update. In R. B. Ruddell, M. R. Ruddell, & H. Singer (Eds.), *Theoretical models and processes of reading* (pp. 323–358). Newark, DE: International Reading Association.

Samuels, S. J., Schermer, N., & Reinking, D. (1992). Reading fluency: Techniques for making decoding automatic. In S. J. Samuels & A. E. Farstrup, *What research has to say about reading instruction* (pp. 124–144). Newark, DE: International Reading Association.

Chall, J. (1983). *Stages in reading development*. New York: McGraw-Hill.

Adams, M. J. (1990). *Beginning to read: Thinking and learning about print*. Cambridge, MA: MIT Press.

Johnston, F. (2001). The utility of phonic generalizations: Let's take another look at Clymer's conclusions. *Reading Teacher*, 55 (2), 132–143.

Moustafa, M., & Maldonado-Colon, E. (1999). Whole-to-parts phonics instruction: Building on what children know to help them know more. *Reading Teacher*, 52 (5), 448–458.

Allen, L. (1998) An integrated strategies approach: Making word identification instruction work for beginning readers. *Reading Teacher* 52 (3), 254–268.

Allington, R. L. (2001). *What really matters for struggling readers: Designing research-based programs*. New York: Addison-Wesley Educational Publishers.

Comprehension

Anderson, R. C., & Pearson, P. D. (1984). A schema-theoretic view of basic processes in reading. In P. D. Pearson (Ed.), *Handbook of reading research* (pp. 255–292). White Plains, NY: Longman.

Jones, B. F., Palincsar, A. S., Ogle, D. D., & Carr, E. G. (1987). *Learning and thinking. Stragic teaching and learning: Cognitive instruction in the content areas*. Alexandria, VA: Association for Supervision and Curriculum Development.

Cooper, J. D. (1993). *Literacy: Helping children construct meaning*. Boston: Houghton Mifflin.

Perfetti, C. A. (1985). *Reading ability*. New York: Oxford University Press.

Allington, R. L. (2001). *What really matters for struggling readers: Designing research-based programs*. New York: Addison-Wesley Educational Publishers.

Pearson, P. D., Roehler, L. R., Dole, J. A., & Duffy, G. (1992). Developing expertise in reading comprehension. In S. J. Samuels & A. E. Farstrup, *What research has to say about reading instruction* (pp. 145–199). Newark, DE: International Reading Association.

Taylor, B. M. (1992). Text structure, comprehension and recall. In S. J. Samuels & A. E. Farstrup, *What research has to say about reading instruction* (pp. 220–235). Newark, DE: International Reading Association.

Dowhower, S. L. (1999). Supporting a strategic stance in the classroom: A comprehension framework for helping teachers help students to be strategic. *Reading Teacher*, 52 (7), 672–688.

Villaume, S. K., & Brabham, E. G. (2002). Comprehension instruction: Beyond strategies. *Reading Teacher*, 55 (7), 672–675.

McLaughlin, M. (2003). *Guided comprehension in the primary grades*. Newark, DE: International Reading Association.

Keene, E. O., & Zimmermann, S. (1997). *Mosaic of thought*. Portsmouth, NH: Heinemann.

Writing

Cooper, J. D. (1993). *Literacy: Helping children construct meaning*. Boston: Houghton Mifflin.

Allington, R. L. (2001). *What really matters for struggling readers: Designing research-based programs*. New York: Addison-Wesley Educational Publishers.

Gentry, J. R. (1984). Developmental aspects of learning to spell. *Academic Therapy*, 20, 11–19.

Graves, D. H. (1983). *Writing: Teachers and children at work*. Portsmouth, NH: Heinemann.